Collins Easy Learning Grammar and Punctuation is suitable for everyone who wants to improve their English. Whether you are preparing for exams, need a quick look-up guide to English grammar and punctuation, or you simply want to browse and find out more about the English language and how it works, this book offers you the information you require in a clear and accessible format.

The book begins with a clear outline of the different parts of speech, and goes on to describe their different forms and uses. All the main tenses of English are explained and exemplified, with emphasis on their function in everyday English.

Next, you will find a description of different types of statement and clause, with attention given to structures such as question forms, conditionals, and reported speech. A guide to punctuation gives you clear and up-to-date information on important topics such as the use of the apostrophe, capital letters, and full stops.

Collins' belief in the importance of representing real English remains at the heart of all our descriptions of the language. The Collins Corpus is a 4.5-billion-word database containing up-to-date English from thousands of different spoken and written sources. These include everyday conversations, formal spoken English, newspapers, fiction, and blogs.

This corpus forms the basis of each grammar item, helping us to make confident and accurate decisions about how English grammar works in today's world. Explanations are fully illustrated with examples which remain close to the corpus, occasionally with small changes made so that they can be as clear and helpful as possible.

Finally, we have used our extensive experience in language teaching and learning to identify typical problems that people experience with English grammar. We draw attention to some of the commonest errors, and give tips to help you avoid them. These include issues such as misuse of the apostrophe, over-use of exclamation marks, and incorrect use of important words.

We hope you enjoy finding out more about this important area of the English language. For more information on products to help you improve your English, please visit us at **www.collinselt.com**.

Penny Hands, 2015

contents

contents

contents

Grammar

Parts of speech

Sentences are made up of **words**. A sentence can be made up of any number of words.

> He left us.
> The man in the corner lowered his newspaper.
> Whenever I see Tammy I worry about how I look.
> Until tomorrow then.
> Yes.

We can put words together in many ways to make new sentences.

> I can help you.
> Can I help you?

Grammar describes how we put words together. Each word in a sentence belongs to a particular set or **class**, depending on how it is used. These classes are called **parts of speech**.

All sentences begin with a capital letter and end in either a full stop, a question mark, or an exclamation mark. When we talk about these marks, e.g. commas, semicolons, full stops, brackets, and so on, we are talking about **punctuation**.

The term **clause** is used to describe a group of words that contains a **verb**, the **subject** of that verb, and, often, some other words such as an **object**.

> I live in Sussex.
> ...where I live.
> Jessica lived in Manchester at first.
> He was living in Rome that year.
> ...when he had eaten breakfast.

A sentence can contain one or more **clauses**.

> *I can help you **if you will let me**.*
> ***Whenever you need to talk to someone**, just pop in and see*
> ***if I'm here**.*

Many sentences are made up of a single clause. Single clause sentences are called **simple** sentences.

> *He arrived on Friday.*
> *My brother loves his skateboard.*

A clause always contains a **verb**.

> *run*   *walk*
> *think*   *believe*

A sentence, however, does not always have to be a clause. See p. 258 for more about clauses.

> *Certainly not.*
> *Until tomorrow then.*
> *Yes.*
> *Why?*

A **phrase** is just a **group** of words. The term is usually kept for words which go together naturally.

> *the other day*
> *my friend Henry*
> *in spite of*
> *over the hill*
> *would have been walking*

Many words can refer to one thing only or to more than one. We use the terms **singular** and **plural** for this. A more general term is **number**. Pronouns and nouns can be singular or plural in grammatical number. See p. 200.

When we want to identify the speaker or the person spoken about in grammar, we use **first person** to mean the speaker, **second person** to mean the person who is spoken to, and **third person** to mean the person who is spoken about. For example, we talk about 'first person plural' or 'third person singular'.

pronouns	singular	plural
1st person 2nd person 3rd person	*I* *you* *he, she, it*	*we* *you* *they*
nouns	*the man* *a girl*	*the men* *two girls*

A **verb** tells us about an action or a state of being. Ordinary verbs are called **main verbs**.

come	*go*	*think*
want	*economize*	*believe*

A main verb is sometimes called a 'doing word'. A special group of verbs are called **auxiliary verbs**. These can be put together with main verbs to form different tenses.

> I **am** thinking.
> She **has** seen the film already.
> I **can** help you.
> We **might** need to.

A **noun** is a word that labels a thing or an idea. Nouns are sometimes called 'naming words'.

table	*book*	*ugliness*
time	*animal*	*thing*

If we do not want to repeat the same noun in a sentence or a paragraph we can replace it with a **pronoun**. A pronoun is a word that is used instead of a noun phrase or a noun.

> Gary saw Sue so **he** asked **her** to help him.
> Ross was hungry so **he** stopped at a burger bar.

An **adjective** gives more information about a noun. Adjectives help us describe or pick out which particular thing among many is being referred to. Adjectives are sometimes called 'describing words'.

> a man a **tall** man
> their TV their **new wide-screen** TV
> the cat the **fat black-and-white** cat

A **determiner** is used to point more precisely to the person, thing, or idea that is being talked about. Examples of determiners are **definite** and **indefinite articles** and **possessives**.

> **the** cat **a** man
> **my** aunt **their** TV

An **adverb** gives information about the way that an action is carried out or when and where it takes place.

> She ran **quickly** down the path.
> The children laughed **hysterically**.
> He lifted the box **carefully**.

Some adverbs can also be used before adjectives,

> He was a **rather** tall man.
> This cake is **quite** nice.
> It was **fairly** good.
> It's a **very** hot day.

or to introduce a sentence. Many adverbs are formed from adjectives by adding -ly.

> **Fortunately**, the rain stayed away.
> **Honestly**, I can't help it.

A **preposition** is one of a small group of words that can be used with nouns and verbs. Prepositions give information about position or movement.

> **on** the bridge   **over** the rooftops
> **in** the morning   **at** the gates

When a preposition is used in front of a noun, the two together do the work of an adverb.

> He is coming **now**.
> He is coming **in the morning**.
> I found him **there**.
> I found him **near the gates**.

A **conjunction** joins two or more nouns or clauses to each other. Conjunctions are sometimes called 'joining words'.

> I went to the shop **and** bought some bread.
> I bought some bread, **but** I forgot to get the milk.

Many words can act as more than one part of speech. It is not unusual for an English word to be a **noun** in one sentence and a **verb** in another sentence.

> Jamal scored several **runs**.
> She **runs** half a mile each morning.
> I've been chosen for the school **play**.
> Christopher and Angus **play** golf together on Fridays.

Parts of the sentence

Sentences consist of a number of parts, using different parts of speech. The most important parts of speech are:

- The **subject**, which is either a noun phrase (see p. 133) or a pronoun (see p. 200). Normally the subject comes before the verb phrase in a sentence.

  > *The girls* had been swimming.
  > *The new teacher* came in.
  > *They* had finished.

- The **verb phrase**, which includes the main verb and which may have auxiliary verbs to go with it. See also pp. 28–87.

  > The girls *had been swimming*.
  > The new teacher *came* in.
  > They *had finished*.
  > She *uses* her skateboard quite a lot.
  > Rajiv *was reading* a new novel.
  > She *is riding* someone else's horse.

- The **object**, which is a noun phrase or a pronoun.

  > She used *her old skateboard*.
  > Rajiv was reading *a new novel*.
  > Josh found *it*.

Not all verbs need an object. When there is one, the object normally comes after the verb phrase. Some verbs may also need an **indirect object**. See also p. 228.

> Hamish gave **me** *a party invitation*.
> Ruth gave **Lauren** *a nice bunch of flowers*.

- An **adverbial**, or **adjunct**, which is an optional part of the sentence.

This may be:

- a single word, an **adverb**.

  > **Suddenly**, it started to rain **heavily**.

- an **adverbial phrase**, a group of words that functions as an adverb.

  > **In the morning**, the sky was clear.
  > You probably won't notice it **after a while**.

- an **adverbial clause**, a group of words including a verb, which functions as an adverb.

  > I'll get some biscuits for you **when I've poured the drinks**.
  > **When I've poured the drinks**, I'll get some biscuits for you.
  > Mark played **while Isabel sang**.

Though some adverbials have a fixed position, most can be added to a sentence in several places. Any number of them can be added, limited only by the sense of the sentence.

> **In the winter**, the roads get very slippery.
> The roads get very slippery **in the winter**.

- A **complement**. With certain verbs, such as *be* and *seem*, a complement takes the place of an object. A complement can be either an adjective or a noun phrase. Complements provide further descriptive detail about the subject. See also p. 230.

  > He became **a doctor** in 2005.
  > Andrew is **a motor-mechanic**.
  > He felt **a bit silly** when he realized what he'd done.
  > They became **good friends** despite the mistake.

Direct and indirect objects

The **object** of a sentence (if there is one) normally comes after the verb phrase. Whether there is an object or not depends on the meaning of the verb. For example, if you want to talk about what someone is doing, you might say '*She is writing*' but if you want to talk about the point of the activity, you might say, '*She is writing a book*'.

> *She was riding.*
> *She was riding **her horse**.*
> *Erica was writing.*
> *Erica was writing **a letter**.*

An object that follows a verb like this is called the **direct object**.

> *Rory found **a pen**.*
> *Our cat doesn't like **milk**.*

Some verbs also have another sort of object, called an **indirect object**. An indirect object names the person for or to whom something is done. It is usually needed with verbs like *give*, *find* and *owe*. For example, with *give*, we need to name both the thing that is given and the person it is given to.

> *Mike owes **Tom** five pounds.*
> *Rob gave **me** a box of chocolates.*
> *Susan bought **her rabbit** some more food.*

Some verbs must always take a direct object, some never take a direct object; others sometimes take one and sometimes don't, depending on the meaning. When a verb has an object it is called a **transitive** verb.

> *Rowan bought **a magazine**.*
> *I don't like **rap music**.*

When it does not have an object it is called an **intransitive** verb.

> *Lynn fainted.*
> *Patrick screamed.*
> *Soon, everyone was shouting.*

Some verbs may be either **transitive** or **intransitive**.

> *Ann was reading (a letter).*
> *Kim was drawing (a picture).*

When a verb has both an indirect and a direct object it is called a **ditransitive** verb.

> *Amy owes* **Mark** *ten pounds*.
> *Stephen gave* **me** *some flowers*.
> *Katie bought* **her hamster** *a new cage*.

A direct object is needed where the meaning of the verb requires something to give it a focus. This is why we sometimes say that a direct object 'complements' a verb.

• Some verbs must have an adverbial as well as a direct object, for example to specify a place.

> *He placed* **the parcel** *on the chair*.
> *She put* **the umbrella** *in a corner*.

Verbs

Verbs are words that allow us to talk about activities, processes, states of being, and states of mind.

> This basket **holds** quite a lot.
> John **was reading** Katherine's essay.
> Fiona **is preparing** a talk for next week's class.
> Helen **feels** much happier now.
> I **forgot** that it **was** your birthday.
> Paul **owned** several old motorbikes.

Verbs can be divided into two major groups, according to the way they are used. Those in the larger group are called **main verbs**. The rest are called **auxiliary verbs**.

Verb phrase

A verb phrase can be a single word or a group of associated words.

> he **walks**
> he **is walking**
> he **had walked**
> he **can walk**
> he **has been walking**
> he **might have been walking**

When a verb phrase consists of a single word it is called a **simple** verb. Many verbs in English are made by combining an auxiliary verb and a main verb; this is called a **compound** verb.

- When we want to talk about everything to do with a verb, we use the term **verb phrase**.

Main verbs

These are the verbs that we use to indicate actions and states. Most of the verbs in English are main verbs. They are also called **lexical** verbs. Main verbs are divided or **classified** in several ways:

– according to whether they refer to **states**

> I *can* really *taste* the herbs in this omelette.
> This scarf *belongs* to me.
> He *hates* losing.
> She always *liked* boats and sailing.
> I already *feel* that I *have known* you for ages.

or **actions**.

> Three boys *were kicking* a ball around in the field.
> We *were running* across the football field.
> For six hours, Stuart *drove* across open desert.

– into **regular** and **irregular** verbs according to the spelling of their forms.

> regular: talk, talks, talking, talked.
> irregular: swim, swims, swimming, swam, swum.
> irregular: go, goes, going, went, gone.

– according to whether or not they are followed by an object. That is, whether they are **transitive** or **intransitive**. See p. 81.

> I *can read*.
> We both *read* **the same newspaper**.
> *Don't tell* me.
> We both *ran* away.
> Sue *found* **a bracelet**.
> I *saw* **my best friend** on Friday.

Auxiliary verbs

These verbs are used in combination with main verbs in order to allow us to talk about different times or periods of time, different degrees of completion, and different amounts of certainty or doubt. There are several types of auxiliary verb. The **primary** auxiliaries help express time, and the **modal** auxiliaries help to express certainty and doubt. See pp. 35–74.

Tense

We use verbs to talk about actions and states. Verbs **tenses** allow us to talk about the time when the action or state takes place.

All main verbs have two **simple** tenses, the **present simple** and the **past simple**.

present simple	past simple
I walk she sings they come you bring	I walked she sang they came you brought

In these tenses the verb is used on its own without any auxiliary verbs.

English verbs also have **compound** tense forms. In these tenses the main verb is accompanied by one or both of the auxiliary verbs *be* and *have*. See p. 88 for more on tenses.

Aspect

The compound tenses of the verb express two **aspects** – **continuous** and **perfect**.

- The term **aspect** is used to talk about continuing actions versus completed actions or states. Simple tenses do not have aspect.

continuing actions	
I am walking she is singing they are coming you are bringing	I was walking she was singing they were coming you were bringing

completed actions	
I have walked *she has sung* *they have come* *you have brought*	*I had walked* *she had sung* *they had come* *you had brought*

We use these compound verbs when we want to talk about:

– the continuous nature of an action (using a form of the auxiliary
be + *-ing*). This is called the **continuous aspect**.

> *I **am** still **studying** French.*
> *He **was living** in London all that year.*
> *James **is helping out** with the children this week.*
> *Sara and Scott **were looking** for a new flat at the time.*

– the completion of an action (using a form of the auxiliary
have + a past participle, usually *-ed*). This is called the **perfect
aspect**.

> *I **have been** a teacher for four years.*
> *He **had lived** in London for a year before coming to Sussex.*
> *James **has helped out** before.*
> *Sara and Scott **had found** their flat by then.*

The two aspects of the verb can be joined so that we can talk about
the duration and the completion of an action in the same verb phrase.
See pp. 88–89 for more on tense and aspect.

> *I **have been studying** French for four years.*
> *I **had been living** in London for four years when I met him.*
> *James **has been helping** us this week.*

Simple tenses

Simple tenses show moments in time, timeless states, and habitual or repetitive actions.

> It **tastes** good.
> Julie **keeps** a diary.
> Adrian **went** home at midnight.
> She **heard** a strange noise in the night.
> Rob usually **walks** to school.
> Yesterday he **went** by car.

The **present simple** and the **past simple** of regular verbs are formed by using the base form of the verb. See pp. 94–97.

Continuous tenses

Continuous tenses show duration or continuity.

> It **is raining** hard this morning.
> It **was raining** when we came out of school yesterday.
> I'm **having** dinner. Can I call you back?
> He **was listening** to the radio when he heard the news.

The **present continuous** and the **past continuous** are formed from either the present or the past tense of the verb *be* + the **present participle** (or '*-ing* form') of the main verb. See pp. 98–101.

Perfect tenses

The present perfect tense shows that an action is completed but that it still has some importance in the present time.

> Ken **has walked** all the way from the station. (...and he's tired.)
> He **has** never **visited** me. (...and I'm feeling neglected.)
> She **has missed** the train. (That's why she's not here.)

The **past perfect** is used to talk about something that happened in a time before a particular time in the past.

> He told us that he **had tried** it before.
> I **had** never **been** climbing before our activity holiday last year.
> She was late because she **had missed** her train.

The **present perfect** and the **past perfect** are formed using either the present or the past tense of the verb **have** + **the past participle** of the main verb. See pp. 102–105.

Perfect continuous tenses

Perfect continuous tenses show duration, completion, and importance in the present time.

> I **have been working** hard in the garden all day.
> My mother **has been helping** me.
> My sisters **have been riding** all day.
> I **had been working** in Italy that summer.
> Some of us **had been waiting** for two hours when the
>   doctor appeared.

The **present perfect continuous** and the **past perfect continuous** are formed using either the present or past tense of the verb **have** + **the past participle** of **be** + **the present participle** of the main verb. See p. 106.

Other verb forms

Other verb combinations are used for positive or negative statements,
or to express degrees of time and probability.

> *Do you **like** espresso coffee?*
> *I **don't** **like** fried food.*
> ***Could** I **have** a coke, please?*
> *You **will be** in Edinburgh within two hours.*
> *They **will** probably **meet** us at the station.*

Types of main verb

Verbs of action

Most verbs describe an action such as *walking, running,* or *reading*.

> John **is running** for the train.
> Sophie **has** just **bought** a new camera.
> She **is putting on** an exhibition of her photographs.
> Robbie **has seen** the film already.

When we need a verb to describe a new activity, we can either invent a new word, or we can adapt other parts of speech.

> You can use your phone to **access** the internet.

- Action verbs can be expressed in all the tenses.

Verbs of state

Some verbs are used to talk about states of being or states of mind.

These include:

- verbs relating to the senses, e.g. *feel, hear, see, smell, taste*
- verbs relating to emotions, e.g. *adore, fear, hate, like, love, want, wish*
- verbs relating to mental activity, e.g. *agree, believe, expect, forget, mean*
- verbs relating to possession, e.g. *belong, own, possess*

> I **feel** unhappy.
> I **hate** arguments.
> These flowers **smell** gorgeous.
> Rob **wishes** he hadn't **agreed** to the plan.
> We **mean** you no harm.
> That car **belonged** to us once.

- Verbs of state are not usually used in continuous tenses. When they are used in continuous tenses, they change their meaning.

    *I'm just **feeling** to see if the bone is broken.*
    *We **were tasting** some interesting New Zealand wines.*
    *Naomi **is expecting** a baby.*

There are some uses of the verb **be** that allow you to choose between a state or an action meaning. The word used as the complement makes an important difference.

*Mark **is being** silly*	**but not** *Mark is being tall.*
*Oscar **is being** nasty*	**but not** *Oscar is being intelligent.*

The verb **seem** has a limited number of adjectives that can be used as its complement.

*Simon seems **happy***	**but not** *Simon seems tall.*

The forms of main verbs

English verbs have up to five different forms. These are:

1 the base form, e.g. **_pull_**
2 the 3rd person singular, present simple tense, e.g. **_pulls_**
3 the past simple tense, e.g. **_pulled_**
4 the past participle, e.g. **_pulled_**
5 the present participle, e.g. **_pulling_**

- Regular verbs are all formed in the same way, by building on the **base form** (form 1). This is the form you normally find in a dictionary. Most verbs are regular.

- Irregular verbs have different forms, particularly forms 3 and 4. See p. 32.

Form 1:   The **present simple** tense has all but one of its forms the same as the **base form**.

Form 2:   When the **present simple** tense has a 3rd person singular subject, the verb is formed from the **base form** + **-s**.

Form 3:   The **past simple** is formed from the **base form** + **-ed**.

Form 4:   The **past participle** is formed from the **base form** + **-ed**.

Form 5:   The **present participle** is formed from the **base form** + **-ing**.

A special variation of the base form is the **_to_ infinitive**. There are a number of uses of a verb where both the words **_to_** + the **base form** must be present.

> The base form is sometimes called the 'bare infinitive'.

As mentioned above, the 3rd person singular is formed from the **base form** + **-s**. Below are the exceptions to the rule:

Verbs ending in **-o**, **-ch**, **-sh**, **-ss**, **-x**, **-z** or **-zz**: add **-es** to make the 3rd person singular, e.g.

torpedo	he torpedo**es**
catch	he catch**es**
toss	he toss**es**
push	he push**es**
miss	he miss**es**
box	he box**es**
buzz	it buzz**es**

Verbs ending in **-y** after a consonant: change **y** to **i** and add **-es**, e.g.

carry	he carr**ies**
fly	he fl**ies**
worry	he worr**ies**

As mentioned above, the present participle is made up of the **base form** + **-ing**. There are some exceptions to the rule. All verbs that contain a short final vowel in front of a final consonant double the consonant before **-ing**, e.g.

sob	sobbing
bid	bidding
flog	flogging
run	running
stop	stopping
get	getting
put	putting

Irregular verbs

Irregular verbs are verbs that *do not* form the past simple tense and the past participle by adding *-ed* to the base form.

The three main groups of irregular verbs

In Group A, the base form, the past simple and the past participle are the same:

1 the base form   **put**
2 the present simple tense   *puts*
3 the past simple tense   **put**
4 the present participle   *putting*
5 the past participle   **put**

A				
bet	*cut*	*let*	*set*	*spread*
burst	*hit*	*put*	*shed*	*thrust*
cast	*hurt*	*shut*	*split*	*upset*

In Group B, the past simple and the past participle have the same form:

1 the base form   **buy**
2 the present simple tense   *buys*
3 the past simple tense   **bought**
4 the present participle   *buying*
5 the past participle   **bought**

B1

base form	past form	base form	past form
bend	bent	hang	hung
bind	bound	have	had
bleed	bled	hear	heard
bring	brought	keep	kept
build	built	kneel	knelt
buy	bought	lay	laid
catch	caught	make	made
find	found	say	said

Some of these verbs have alternative spellings for the past participle:

B2 The past form may be either *a* or *b*.

base form	past forms		base form	past forms	
burn	burnt	burned	smell	smelt	smelled
dream	dreamt	dreamed	spell	spelt	spelled
lean	leant	leaned	spill	spilt	spilled
learn	learnt	learned	spoil	spoilt	spoiled

In Group C, the base form, the past simple, and the past participle all have different forms:

1 the base form **go**
2 the present simple tense *goes*
3 the past simple tense **went**
4 the present participle *going*
5 the past participle **gone**

C

base form	past forms		base form	past forms	
arise	arose	arisen	ring	rang	rung
awake	awoke	awoken	rise	rose	risen
bear	bore	borne	saw	sawed	sawn
begin	began	begun	see	saw	seen
bite	bit	bitten	shake	shook	shaken
blow	blew	blown	show	showed	shown
break	broke	broken	shrink	shrank	shrunk
fly	flew	flown	strive	strove	striven
give	gave	given	take	took	taken
know	knew	known	throw	threw	thrown
ride	rode	ridden	write	wrote	written

Auxiliary verbs

An auxiliary verb is a verb that is used together with a main verb to show time and continuity.

- **Be** and **have** are the **primary auxiliaries**. A primary auxiliary is used to construct compound tenses.

- **Be** is used to make present continuous and past continuous tenses

  > I **am working**.
  > Rob **is using** the computer.
  > We **were** all **wondering** about that.
  > Kevin **was teaching** in America in 1995.

  and also for the passive. See p. 40 for more on **be**.

  > These books **are sold** in supermarkets.
  > Martin **was arrested** and held overnight.

- **Have** is used to make present perfect and past perfect tenses. See p. 44 for more on *have*.

  > Stephen **has finished** fixing the car.
  > George and Alice **have seen** the show already.
  > Amanda **had** already **eaten** when we arrived.
  > They **had** not **expected** to see us there.

- **Do** is the **supporting auxiliary**. It is used in forming negatives, questions, and emphatic statements. See p. 48 for more on **do**. See pp. 88–93 for more on simple and compound verb forms.

  > I **do** not **like** sausages at all.
  > **Do** you **like** prawns?
  > You **do like** prawns, don't you?

- *Will*, *may*, *might*, and the other verbs listed on pp. 53–54 are the **modal auxiliary verbs**, usually called simply, **modal verbs**. A modal verb allows us to talk about actions as possible, doubtful, or necessary.

> Charlie **will go** home on Friday.
> Charlie **may go** home on Friday.
> Charlie **could go** home on Friday.
> Charlie **must go** home on Friday.

Auxiliaries can be combined together in a single verb phrase. For example, a verb phrase may consist of a **modal** + a form of *have* + a form of *be* + a form of a **main verb**.

> I **could have been making** a bad mistake by trusting him.
> Sara **will have been living** in New Zealand for 2 years
>   next month.
> You **must have been given** the wrong number.

The auxiliary verb, or if there is more than one of them, the first auxiliary verb, performs these following grammatical functions:

– It shows **tense** and is the **finite** part of the verb phrase.

> I **have** seen it.
> She **had** seen it.
> She **has** been thinking.
> She **had** been thinking.

– It shows **number** and **person** agreement with the subject.

> **She has** seen it.
> **They have** seen it.
> **I am** looking for it.
> **You are** looking for it.

– It will take any **negative** immediately after it.

> I **do not** want to do that.
> She **has not** been concentrating.

– It can come before the subject to make a **question**.

> **Do you** want to help us?
> **Have you** got a mobile phone?

Contracted forms

Auxiliaries are very often used in contracted forms. In the case of **be** and **have**, the contracted form can involve linking the subject and the auxiliary verb into a single form e.g. *I'm, I've, we'd, Sue's (Sue has or Sue is).*

> **We're** back!
> **(We are** back!)
> **I've** found it.
> **(I have** found it.)
> **They'd** gone when I got there.
> **(They had** gone when I got there.)
> **Tom's** here.
> **(Tom is** here.)

The contracted negative form **auxiliary** + **n't** is common with all the auxiliaries except *am*, e.g. *hasn't, wouldn't, don't.*

> She **isn't** (is not) trying.
> We **don't** (do not) live here.
> He **hasn't** (has not) seen it.
> I **can't** (cannot) come.

In standard British English, the contracted form of **am not**, when it is part of a question, is **aren't I**.

> **Aren't I** *going to need some matches?*
> *I'm getting a lift with you,* **aren't I**?

- Contracted forms are more informal than full forms. They are therefore more common in spoken English. Full forms are usually preferred in formal written English.

Auxiliaries are used in sentence tags. See p. 241 for more about sentence tags.

> *You had only just bought that carpet when the kitchen flooded,*
>   **hadn't you**?
> *It's Katie's birthday on Saturday,* **isn't it**?
> *You are joking,* **aren't you**?

Auxiliaries are also used to make a short addition to a statement, such as:

- a positive addition to a positive statement, accompanied by *so* or *too*.

> *I went to the park and Lucy* **did too**.
> *I loved the film, and* **so did** *Finlay*.

- a negative addition to a negative statement, accompanied by *neither* or *nor*.

> *My dad never eats mussels and* **neither do** *I*.
> *I don't want to speak to William now. –* **Nor do** *I*.
> *I can't understand it. –* **Neither can** *I*.

- Auxiliaries can be used in positive sentences to give emphasis. When they are emphatic they are never contracted.

  You **have** made a mess!
  That **was** a nice surprise!
  I **am** proud of Katie. She's so clever.

  In the present simple tense and the past simple tenses the appropriate form of **do** is used to show emphasis.

  I **do like** Penny. – So do I.
  We **did have** a lovely time.

An auxiliary on its own can be used to give a short answer to a question. Whatever auxiliary is used in the question is used on its own in the answer. The main verb is not repeated. Short answers are very common in spoken English.

Do you like avocados? Yes, I **do**. or No, I **don't**.
Have you read anything by Michael Morpurgo?
    Yes, I **have**.

Be

The verb *be* is used as an auxiliary verb and it can also be used as a main verb. See p. 28.

The verb *be* is irregular. It has eight different forms: *be*, *am*, *is*, *are*, *was*, *were*, *being*, *been*. The present simple and past simple tenses make more changes than those of other verbs.

> I *am* late.
> You *are* late.
> He *is* late.

> We *are* late.
> You *are* late.
> They *are* late.

> I *was* late.
> You *were* late.
> She *was* late.

> We *were* late.
> You *were* late.
> They *were* late.

The present participle is *being*.

> He is *being* very helpful these days.

The past participle is *been*.

> We have *been* ready for an hour.

- The present simple tense forms of *be* are often contracted in normal speech. Note that the contracted form of *they are* is spelled *they're*, and not *their* which is the possessive form of *they*.

> I'm here.
> You're here.
> He's here.

> We're here.
> You're here.
> They're here.

Any form of *be* is made negative by adding *not* immediately after it. In speech, some forms of *be* also have contracted negative forms. Some of these forms emphasize the negative.

	emphasizes the negative
I**'m not** late. You **aren't** late. He **isn't** late. We **aren't** late. They **aren't** late.	You**'re not** late. He**'s not** late. We**'re not** late. They**'re not** late.
I **wasn't** late. You **weren't** late. He **wasn't** late. We **weren't** late. They **weren't** late.	

The major uses of **be** as an auxiliary verb are to form continuous tenses and the passive.

- **Continuous** tenses of main verbs use the appropriate form of **be**, present or past, followed by the present participle (or **-ing** form). See p. 98 and p. 106.

- The **passive** form of a main verb uses the appropriate form of **be** followed by the past participle. See p. 118.

The verb **be** is also used as a main verb. It is commonly found joining a subject to its complement.

As a **main verb**, **be** is used to talk about:

- Feelings and states. For this we use the simple tenses of the verb with a suitable adjective. See p. 88.

    I **am delighted** with the news but he **is not happy**.
    She **was busy** so she **was not able** to see me.

- People's behaviour. For this we use the continuous tenses of the verb with a suitable adjective. See p. 96.

    > I **am not being** slow, I **am being** careful.
    > You **were being** very rude to your mum when I came downstairs.

- **Be** + the **to infinitive** is sometimes used to refer to future time. This is a rather formal use, which often appears in news reports. See pp. 128–132.

    > The Prime Minister **is to visit** Hungary in October.
    > The Archbishop **is to have** talks with the Pope next month.

- **It** + **be**: we use **it** as a subject when we are talking about time, distance, weather, or cost. In this use, **be** is always singular.

    > Hurry up, **it's eight thirty**!
    > **Is it**? I didn't know **it was so late**.

    > **It's** thirty miles to Glasgow.
    > Come and visit us. **It's not very far**.

    > **It's cold** today but **it isn't wet**.

    > **It's very expensive** to live in London.

- **There** + **is/are** is used to talk about something existing. In this use, the form that **be** takes may be singular or plural, depending on the number of the noun, and **be** is sometimes contracted.

    > **There's** a spare toothbrush in the cupboard.
    > **There was** a cold wind blowing.
    > **There isn't** enough petrol for the journey.
    > **There are** several petrol stations on the way, **aren't there**?

To make the continuous tenses of the main verb **be** we have to use **be** twice, once as an auxiliary and once as a main verb.

> You **are being** so annoying!
> I know I **am being** silly, but I am frightened.

The question form of clauses with the verb **be** in them is made by putting the appropriate form of **be** right in front of the subject.

> **Are you** better now?
> **Is he** free this morning?
> **Was he** cooking dinner when you arrived?

Have

The verb *have* is used as an auxiliary verb

> She *has* run a lovely, deep, bubble bath.
> Katie *had* read about the concert in the newspaper.

and also as a main verb. See p. 24.

> She is *having* a bath at the moment.
> The driver has *had* his breakfast, so we can go.

The verb *have* has the forms: *have*, *has*, *having*, *had*. The base form of the verb is *have*. The present participle is *having*. The past tense and past participle form is *had*.

- The present and past forms are often contracted in everyday speech, especially when *have* is being used as an auxiliary verb.

  The contracted forms are:

have = *'ve*	I*'ve* seen the Queen.
has = *'s*	He*'s* gone on holiday.
	Ian*'s* behaved badly.
had = *'d*	You*'d* better go home.
	Ian*'d* left them behind.

  The form *have* contracts to *'ve*. This can sound rather like *of*, especially after other auxiliary verbs.

  > She *would've* given you something to eat.
  > You *could've* stayed the night with us.
  > If he'd asked, I *might've* lent him my car.

  Avoid the common mistake of writing *of* in this case.

As an **auxiliary** verb, **have** is used to make the **perfect tenses** of main verbs.

The **perfect** tenses of main verbs use the appropriate form of **have**, present or past, followed by the past participle. See pp. 102–109.

> I **have read** *some really good books over the holidays.*
> I **had seen** *the film before.*

The negative of a clause containing a compound verb with **have** is made by adding **not** or another negative word immediately after the appropriate form of **have**. In speech, some forms of **have** also have contracted negative forms.

> I **have never seen** *such luxury.*
> *Rachel* **had not been** *abroad before.*
> *She* **had hardly had** *time to eat when Paul arrived.*

• present tense and past tense forms that emphasize the negative element:

*I/we/you/they***'ve not**;   *he/she/it***'s not**
*I/we/you/he/she/it /they***'d not**

> *She***'s not** *told me about it yet.*
> *We***'ve not** *been here before.*
> *They***'d not** *seen him for weeks.*

• present tense and past tense negative forms that are used less emphatically:

I/we/you/they **haven't**;   *he/she/it* **hasn't**
I/we/you/he/she/it /they **hadn't**

> *He* **hasn't** *found anywhere to stay this holiday.*
> *We* **haven't** *been here before.*
> *They* **hadn't** *looked very hard, in my opinion.*

As a **main verb**, *have* is used to talk about:

- states or conditions, such as possession or relationship.

- In these uses, continuous tenses are not possible. With this meaning *have* is sometimes used alone, adding only *not* to make negatives, and adding nothing to make questions.

> *I have something for you.*
> *We haven't anything for you today.*
> *Have you no sense of shame?*
> *The driver has had his breakfast, so we can go.*
> *We had a good time.*

It is also often used with forms of *do* to make negatives and questions.

> *Do you have a pen?*
> *Does she have my umbrella?*
> *She doesn't have any brothers or sisters.*
> *Do you have time to see me now?*

- *Have got* is an informal form of this main verb use of *have*, often used in speaking, especially in British English.

> *I haven't got any brothers or sisters.*
> *Has she got my umbrella? – Yes, she has.*
> *She hasn't got any money.*

- activities, including those such as eating, and leisure.

With this meaning of *have*, negatives and questions are formed using one of the forms of *do*.

> *He was having a shower when I phoned.*

*I'm **having** lunch at twelve o'clock.*
*Come and **have** a sandwich with me,*
*No thanks. I **don't** usually **have** lunch.*

*He's **having** a day off.*
***Did** you **have** a good holiday?*

Contractions and weak forms are not possible with this meaning.

***Have got** is not used with this meaning.*

- to express obligation using ***have to*** or ***have got to***.

    *I've **got to** go now, I'm afraid.*
    ***Do you have to** leave so soon?*
    ***Have you got to** leave so soon?*

When ***have*** is a main verb, it makes perfect forms like all other main verbs. This means that it is possible to use ***have*** twice in present or past perfect sentences, once as an auxiliary verb and once as a main verb.

*We **have had** enough, thank you.*
*They **had** already **had** several warnings.*

Do

The verb *do* is used as an auxiliary verb.

I **do** not want it.	We **do** not want it.
You **do** not want it.	You **do** not want it.
He **does** not want it.	They **do** not want it.

I **did** not want it.	We **did** not want it.
You **did** not want it.	You **did** not want it.
She **did** not want it.	They **did** not want it.

It can also be used as a main verb. See p. 28. When *do* is used as an auxiliary verb it is a **supporting verb**. Because a main verb cannot combine directly with negatives or make questions, *do* is used to support the main verb.

> **Don't** talk!
> **Don't** run!

It is also used to stand in for another verb to avoid repetition, as shown on p. 39.

The verb *do* is irregular. It has five different forms: *do*, *does*, *doing*, *did*, *done*. The base form of the verb is *do*. The past simple form, *did*, is the same throughout. The present participle is *doing*. The past participle is *done*.

The present simple tense *do* and the past simple tense *did* can be used as an auxiliary verb. As an auxiliary, *do* is not used with **modal** verbs.

I **do** not want it.	We **do** not want it.
You **do** not want it.	You **do** not want it.
He **does** not want it.	They **do** not want it.

I **did** not want it.	We **did** not want it.
You **did** not want it.	You **did** not want it.
She **did** not want it.	They **did** not want it.

As an **auxiliary** verb *do* is used in the following ways:

– to help make the negative and question forms of present simple and past simple tenses.

> *Oh dear, I **didn't feed** the cat this morning.*
> ***Do** you **know** what time it is?*
> ***Did** Tim **pay** for his ticket last night?*

– to make the negative form of a command.

> ***Don't** talk!*
> ***Don't** run!*

– to make a command more persuasive. See p. 246.

> ***Do** let me see it!*

– to avoid repeating a main verb in additions, commands, sentence tags, and short answers.

> *They often go to the cinema, **and so do** we.*

> *Don't run on the road! Don't **do** it!*

> *You live in Glasgow, **don't** you?*

> *Do you play cricket? – No, I **don't**.*
> *Did they tell you the news? – Yes, they **did**.*
> *Jim likes jazz, I think. Yes, **he does**.*

– in comparisons.

>   She **sings** better than I **do**.

The positive forms of **do** cannot be contracted. In speech, the negative has contracted forms.

>   I **don't** (do not) agree with you.
>   She **doesn't** (does not) live here now.
>   They **didn't** (did not) buy any food.

- present tense negative forms:
  I/we/you/they **don't**; he/she/it **doesn't**

- past tense negative form:
  I/we/you/he/she/it/they **didn't**

When **do** is a main verb, it has a range of meanings that includes *carry out*, *perform*, *fix*, or *provide*. It is sometimes used in place of a more specific verb.

>   I'll **do** the lawn now.
>   (I'll **mow** the lawn now.)
>   I'll **do** you.
>   (I'll **punch** you.)
>   We don't **do** coach parties.
>   (We don't **serve** coach parties.)

It is then used with the full range of tenses and forms. See also p. 94.

>   **Are** you **doing** your homework?
>   You **have been doing** well this term.
>   She **had done** enough, so she stopped.
>   This **has been done** before.

The main verb use of **do** can be used to talk about:

– habits.

> I **do** the washing up every evening.
> This what I usually **do**.

– behaviour.

> He **did** something rather foolish.
> I **didn't do** anything wrong.
> What **are** you **doing**?

– plans.

> What **are** you **doing** on Sunday?

As a main verb, **do** makes negatives and questions like all other main verbs:

– in the present simple tense with auxiliary **do**.

> What **does** he **do** for a living?
> **Do** I **do** it this way?
> No, you **don't do** it like that at all.

– in the past simple tense with auxiliary **did**.

> **Did** Henry **do** it, then?
> **Didn't** Henry **do** it, then?
> He **didn't do** it, you know.

This means that it is possible to use **do** twice in negative and interrogative sentences; once as an auxiliary verb and once as a main verb.

- As a main verb, **do** can be used with modal verbs.

    *They **will do** it for you, if you ask nicely.*
    *I **can do** it, but I **shouldn't do** it.*

Modal verbs

Modal verbs are a particular kind of **auxiliary**.

> Look, I **can** do it! – Oh yes! So you **can**.
> **Can** I use your phone? – Of course you **can**.
> Do you think she **will** come? – I'm sure she **will**.
> I **must** get our tickets today.

Modal verbs are used when you need to add special elements of meaning to a main verb, e.g.:

– to express different degrees of doubt and possibility about the action of the main verb.

> I **may** not **be able** to do it.
> I think that I **might have caught** your cold.
> I **could ask** for you, if you like.
> You **couldn't do** it, **could** you?

– to express degrees of future possibility, ranging from the definite future, **will**, to the possible future, **may**, and the conditional future, **could**.

> You **will be seeing** her **on Friday** at Jackie's house.
> I **may be** late home **tomorrow evening**.
> I **could bring** some more bread home with me **tonight**.

– to request or give permission for an action to take place.

> **May** I come in?
> You **can** borrow my car tonight if you like.

– to make a prohibition, when used with a negative.

> You **shouldn't** use this computer without permission.
> You **cannot** borrow my car tonight.
> He **must not** see this letter.

– to speculate.

> *The weather's so bad the flight **could** be late.*
> *It **might** be all over by the time we get there.*
> *He **may** be very cross about all this.*

– to express obligation and duty.

> *I **must** give in my essay today.*
> *Helen **ought to** tell the truth.*

– to refer to typical behaviour.

> *She **can** be very kind on occasions like this.*

– to add politeness to a request which might otherwise sound abrupt.

> ***Would you** please close the door.*

– to make conditional sentences (see p. 273).

– in reported speech (see p. 279).

Modals can refer to a time range that reaches from the immediate present to some future time, so that they can all be used for future reference, especially when they are used with a time adverbial. See pp. 110–117.

> *You **will be seeing** her **on Friday** at Jackie's house.*
> *I **may be** late home **tomorrow evening**.*
> *I **could bring** some more bread home with me **tonight**.*

Some modals can refer to a time range that goes back from the immediate present to some indefinite past time. They can refer to habitual action when they are used with a time adverbial.

> *When I was little, I **would** ride my bike round and round the lawn.*

Form

Unlike other verbs, modal verbs have only one form, the **base form**, and only one tense, the present simple.

> You **will** be seeing her **on Friday** at Jackie's house.
> I **may** be late home **tomorrow evening**.
> I **might** go to visit Grandma **on Saturday**.

They do not have a **to** infinitive. They have no **-s** inflection in the 3rd person singular.

> **He will** be seeing her on Friday.
> **She may** be late home.

- Since modal verbs do not have past tense forms, you have to use other verbs to provide some of the modal meanings in the past, e.g. past necessity is expressed by *had to* instead of *must*.

> I **must** visit Auntie May today.
> I **had to** visit Auntie May yesterday.

- The modals **shall** and **will** are usually contracted to **'ll** in spoken English. All the negative forms can be contracted to form a single word such as **can't**, **won't**, **wouldn't**. These contracted forms are common in both spoken and written English.

> I will/shall = **I'll**
> We will/shall = **we'll**
> You **mustn't** say things like that, Jane.
> John **can't** come to my party.

There are other contracted forms such as **he'll**, **we'll**, **shan't**, and **they'll**, which are common in spoken English but rare in written English.

- Several verbs act as modals sometimes and as full main verbs at other times. These are called **semi-modal verbs**.

> How **dare** he!
> He **dared** to ask me to do his washing!
> She **need**n't come if that's how she feels.
> Monica **needs** a new raincoat.

Position

Modals come before any other auxiliary verb or main verb in the verb phrase.

- Modal verbs are followed by the **base form** of the verb if there is no other auxiliary verb present.

> Yes, you **can borrow** those earrings tonight.
> You **should try** that new restaurant in town.
> You **must come** over again some time.

If one of the auxiliary verbs **have** or **be** follows the modal verb, the main verb will take the appropriate present or past participle form.

> I **may have upset** him.
> You **could have looked** for it yourself.
> Janice **might be coming** too.
> Sue **will have been worried** about her, I imagine.

- In negative sentences, **not** comes immediately after the modal verb and in front of all the other verbs.

> They **may not wait** for you if you're late.
> He **must not be** disturbed after 9 o'clock.

- **Can** cannot be combined with the auxiliary form **have**, but the negative form **can't** can be combined with **have**.

> They **can't have seen** him.　　　　**but not** *They can have seen him.*

Can and could

Both these verbs indicate ability in some respect. The use of *could* is usual in clauses that contain a reference to past time.

> *Morag* **can** *speak French quite well now.*
> *I* **couldn't** *play chess two years ago, but I* **can** *now.*
>
> *When I was younger I* **could** *play tennis really well.*
> *Winston is so strong he* **can** *lift me right off my feet.*
> **Can you** *get up the stairs without help?*
> *You* **can** *come over for dinner whenever you like.*

Can and **could** are used:

– to indicate that you know how to do something.

> *Mary* **can** *do these sums.*
> *I* **couldn't** *draw very well when I was younger.*

– to show ability to do something. (Compared with *be able to*, **can** indicates ability of a more general nature that includes 'is permitted to'.)

> *When I was younger I* **could** *ski really well.*
> *Graham* **can** *run ten miles in 25 minutes.*
> **Are you able to** *walk to the car?*

– to make polite requests or to ask for permission:

> **Could** is more tentative than **can**. (Compare with *may*, which is more formal.)

> **Can** *I borrow the car tomorrow evening, Mum?*
> **Could** *I come with you on the trip?*
> **May** *I take this book home with me?*

– to express the possibility of an action in the future, especially when the possibility is related to plans or projects. (Compare with *may*, where the possibility referred to is still uncertain and in the future.)

> We **can** go to Paris next week since you are free.
> We **could** go to Paris next week if you are free.
> We **may** go to Paris, but it depends on our finances.

– to express the possibility of an action in the present.

> You **can** dive off these rocks; it is quite safe here.
> We **could** dive off the rocks, but we must take care.

– to talk about actions that were possible but did not happen, using **could** + the perfect form of **have**.

> Mary **could have stopped** the fight but she didn't.

– using the perfect form of **have**, to speculate about actions that have recently taken place.

> Who **could/can have broken** the window?
> Who **would have guessed** that they were related?

A distinction between **can** and **could** is observed in conditionals. **Could** is used when the conditions are not met.

> **If** Louisa is coming, she **can** look after the children for a while.
> **If** Helen had more money, she **could** buy a computer.

When changing sentences from direct to reported speech **can** is usually changed to **could**.

> Bernard said, 'I **can** do it for you, Sue.'
> Bernard said that he **could** do it for Sue.

---

can
The negative form is: **cannot**.

> I **cannot** understand why he did it.

The contracted negative form is: **can't**.

> I **can't** help it.

could
The contracted negative form is: **couldn't**.

> I **couldn't** help it.

May and might

Both *may* and *might* can be used in requests and in expressions of possibility for the present and future.

> *Might* I ask you your name?

> The weather **may/might** be better tomorrow.
> Craig **may/might** know his results soon.
> We **may/might** go to the cinema tonight.

> '*May* I come with you?' Nicky asked.
> Nicky asked if she **could** come with them.

May and *might* are used as follows:

– *May* is used to ask permission in a more formal way than *can*.

> *May* I have a drink, please?
> *May* I use your ruler? I've lost mine.

Might is occasionally used in formal situations.

> *Might* I suggest a different solution?

– *May* is used to give permission, particularly when applied to *you, he, she, they* or a proper noun, to show that the speaker is allowing something to happen.

> You **may** go now.
> Users **may** download forms from this website.

– Both *may* and *might* are used to express the possibility of some future action; *might* is more tentative than *may*.

> The weather **may/might** be better tomorrow.
> Craig **may/might** know his results soon.
> We **may/might** go to the cinema tonight.

– **May** is often used for politeness, to make an order appear as a request; **might** is used to make the speaker more remote from the request.

> You **might** give that idea a bit more consideration.
> You **might** want to move a bit closer to the screen.

– **Might** is occasionally used when someone is trying to persuade another person to do something, perhaps with some degree of irritation. This use is a little old-fashioned.

> You **might** give me some cake too, Lucy.
> Anna, come on, you **might** tell me what he said!

• When **might** is used in a conditional sentence, the **if** clause can be in the present or the past tense. Compare with **could**. See p. 58.

> If Louisa **comes**, she **might** look after the children.
> If Louisa **came**, she **might** look after the children.

When changing sentences from direct to reported speech **may** usually becomes **could**.

> '**May** I come with you?' Nicky asked.
> Nicky asked if she **could** come with them.

may
The contracted negative form is: none or **mayn't** (rare).

might
The contracted negative form is: **mightn't**.

> He **mightn't** have enough money.
> We might come and live here, **mightn't** we, mum?

Must

Must is used to express obligation, give orders and give advice. It can only be used for present and future reference. When the past is involved, you use *have to*.

Must is used:

– to express obligation.

> All pupils **must** bring a packed lunch tomorrow.

– to give orders firmly and positively.

> You **must** go to sleep now.

– to give advice or make recommendations emphatically.

> You **must** get one of these new smoothie-makers – they're great!
> You **must** see 'Nim's Island' – it's brilliant.

– to speculate about the truth of something.

> She **must** be mad!
> You **must** be joking!
> There **must** be some mistake.
> Mr Robertson is here; it **must** be Tuesday.

When this sort of statement is made in the negative or interrogative, *can* is used instead.

> **Can** Mary be joking? **Can** she really mean that?
> You **can't** be serious!
> It **can't** be true!

- *Must* can be used in the interrogative, but many speakers prefer *have to* instead.

    > *Must you* go so soon?
    > *Must I* invite Helen?
    > *Do you have to* go soon?
    > *Do I have to* invite Helen?

You can use *must* with a negative:

- to forbid someone to do something.

    > You *must not* cross when the light is red.
    > You *must not* say things like that.

- to talk about an event or state that is unacceptable.

    > There *mustn't* be any mistakes in your letter.
    > The whale *must not* become extinct.

> Note that to express the fact that you are not obliged to do something, you use *do not have to*.
>
> Compare:
>
> > You *must not* come in here.
> > You *don't have to* come in here (if you don't want to).

- It is necessary to change *must* to *have to* when changing sentences from direct to reported speech.

    > 'I *must* fill out those forms this evening,' said Ian.
    > Ian said that he *had to* fill out some forms.

must

The contracted negative form is: **mustn't**.

*You **mustn't** worry so much.*

Shall and will

The normal way to express simple future time in English is using the modal verb *will* followed by the **base form** of a main verb.

> The modal verb *shall* is not used very much in modern English, except in suggestions or offers of help.
>
> *Shall* I help you? *Shall* I cook supper?
> *Shall* we go to the cinema tonight?

Any distinction between *will* and *shall* is difficult to make in spoken English, since the contracted form, *'ll*, is used to mean both *shall* and *will*.

Shall is used:

– with questions involving *I* and *we* when the speaker is making a suggestion or offering help.

> *Shall* I help you? *Shall* I cook supper?
> *Shall* we go to the cinema tonight?

Will is used:

– with *I* and *we* to show intentions and to make promises.

> Don't worry. I **shan't/won't** be late and Helen **won't** be late either.
> We **shall/will** be in touch.
> I **shall/will** try to ensure that you get a good room.

– with *you*, *he*, *she*, *it*, and *they*, to give reassurances.

> He **will** be well treated.
> You **will** have your money next week.

– to insist on something. Full forms are normally used, and are stressed in speech.

> You **will** do what I tell you!
> Jane **will** go to Mary's even if I have to carry her there.

– to make polite requests and to give invitations.

> **Will** you help me look for my purse?
> **Will** you come to lunch on Friday?

– to give orders.

> You **will** finish your work before you watch TV, **won't** you?
> Louisa, **will** you please be quiet!

– to show that someone persists in doing something (full form with stress).

> Oh! Tony **will** keep jogging me when I'm trying to write!
> No wonder you feel sick. You **will** eat chocolate all day long.

– to show prediction.

> The match **will** be finished by now.
> I think it **will** probably rain tomorrow.

will
The contracted form is: **'ll**.

> He**'ll** be home soon.

The contracted negative form is: **won't**.

> Eve **won't** speak to Harriet.

shall

The contracted form is: **'ll**.

The contracted negative form is: **shan't** (used mainly in British English).

> I **shan't** say a word.

Should

The modal verb **should** is used in the following ways:

– to talk about moral obligation. Compare *ought to* on p. 73.

> They **should** do what you suggest.
> People **should** report this sort of thing to the police.
> She suggested we **should** visit Aunty Irene more often.
> Rob insisted that we **should** think of others before
> ourselves.

– to give advice or instructions.

> You **should** undo the top screws first.
> You **should** keep your credit card separate from your chequebook.

– to suggest that something follows on logically from what has just been said.

> They left here at 6 o'clock, so they **should** be home now.

– to show politeness in a conditional clause. This use is used in formal written communication.

> If you **should** decide to go, please contact us.
> **Should** you need more information, please call the manager.

• **Should** can be used with the main verb after certain set expressions such as, *it is a pity that, it is odd that, I am sorry/surprised that.* This is a more formal use than the same expression without **should**.

> It's a pity that this **should** happen.
> I was quite surprised that he **should** be doing a job like that.

- **Should** + the perfect form of the main verb can be used to express regret about something that was done or not done. Compare with *ought to*.

    He **should have stopped** at the red light.
    You **should have told** me you were ill.

- When changing sentences from direct to reported speech, **should** does not change.

    Anna said that I **should** try to relax more.

In formal English, **should** can be used with *I* or *we* in conditional clauses, instead of the more common **would**. This form is usually, but not always, found together with an **if** clause.

    I **should** love to visit Peru **if I had the money**.
    I **should** be very cross **if they didn't give me a certificate**.
    We **should** hate to miss the play.

In this sense, **would** is more common in modern spoken English.

    I **would** love to visit Peru.
    I **would** be very cross if they didn't give me a certificate.
    We **would** hate to miss the play.

should
The contracted negative form is: **shouldn't**.

Would

The modal verb *would* is commonly used as follows:

– to make a polite request.

> **Would** *you mind moving your bag?*
> **Would** *you give me a hand with this ladder, please?*

– to offer something politely.

> **Would** *you* **like** *some tea or coffee?*

– together with *like* as a polite form of *want*.

> *We* **would like** *to see Mr Brown now, please.*
> *My friends* **would like** *to see your garden.*

– to refer to habitual activity in the past, with the meaning of *used to*.

> *I remember Jeff; he* **would** *watch TV all day if you let him.*
> *Jess was a kind girl; she* **would** *always go out of her way to help people.*

– to show that someone persisted in an activity in the past: **would** is sometimes stressed here.

> *John* **would** *keep nagging at her, though I asked him not to.*
> *She* **would** *go on and on until I lost my temper.*

– to express and ask about probability.

> *I saw a girl at the window. Who* **would** *that be?*
> *Oh, that* **would** *be his elder sister!*

- in conditional clauses, usually together with an **if** clause.

> I **would** have taken it if it had been available.
> If you offered me some more I **wouldn't** refuse.
> Brian **would** have phoned the police if it he'd seen the accident.

When changing sentences from direct speech to reported speech, **will** is usually changed to **would**.

> Anna said, 'Raymond **will** help you.'
> Anna said that Raymond **would** help us.
> James said, 'The car **won't** start!'
> James said that the car **wouldn't** start.

would
The contracted form is: **'d**.

> I**'d** have done it too, given the chance.
> We**'d** like to look at the garden.
> He**'d** be very angry if he knew about it.

The contracted negative form is: **wouldn't**.

> Even if he'd known about it, he **wouldn't** have been angry.

Ought to

The use of **ought to** is similar to **should**, but it is much less frequent.

Like **should**, the verb **ought to** does not have a past form. It is only used with reference to the present and the future.

Ought to is rarely used in questions and negatives. When it is, it is confined mainly to formal styles.

In negatives, **not** comes between **ought** and **to**. In questions, the subject comes between **ought** and **to**.

> I **ought not to** have said those things to her.
> **Ought** we **to** make such a sacrifice for the benefit of future generations?

Ought to is used as follows:

– to express an obligation or an expectation that someone should do something.

> You **ought to** listen carefully.
> We **ought to** leave now.
> Lucy **ought to** go by herself.
> People **ought to** be a bit nicer to us.

– to express the likelihood of something happening.

> Annabel **ought to** be here by now.
> The journey **ought to** take about 2 hours.

– **Ought to** + **have** + **past participle of main verb** is used to express regret that something was not done or to reproach someone for doing or not doing something.

*I **ought to have spoken up** earlier. I'm sorry.*
*You **ought to have offered** to help.*
*They **ought to have told** us what to expect.*

- In questions and negatives, **should** is frequently used instead of **ought to** because it sounds more natural.

  ***Ought** I **to** report it to someone in authority?*
  ***Should** I report it to someone in authority?*
  ***Ought** we **to** make a start?*
  ***Should** we make a start?*

ought to
The contracted negative form is: ***oughtn't (to)***.

*Oh dear, we **oughtn't to** have let that happen.*
*Well then she ought to do something about it, **oughtn't** she?*

Dare and need

The two verbs *dare* and *need* have characteristics of both modal verbs and main verbs. Because of this, they are called **semi-modals**. They sometimes behave like modal verbs and do not add **-s** to the form that goes with *he, she,* and *it*. That is, they have no 3rd person singular inflection. They are then followed by the **base form** of a main verb.

> **Need** I **say** more?
> **Dare** I **ask** how the project's going?

The past form **needed** is not used as a modal; **dared** is occasionally used as a modal.

The modal uses of these verbs are all **negatives** or **questions**.

> *Where will you all be today? – **Need** you ask?*
> *You **needn't** come if you're busy.*
> ***Dare** I suggest that we have a rota system?*
> *I **daren't** tell him the truth; he'll go crazy.*

Questions that are formed with *need* and *dare* are often set expressions such as *Need I/you ask?, Dare I suggest…?* and *Need I/we say more?*

Dare and **need** sometimes behave like main verbs with **-s** inflection. In this case they are followed by the **to** infinitive. They can also use the auxiliary **do** and have the whole range of tenses appropriate to a main verb.

> *Louisa **does**n't **need to know**.*
> ***Does** Paul **need to go** now?*
> *Paul **needs to go**.*
> ***Dare to be** different!*
> *I **don't dare to mention** it to him.*

When **dare** or **need** are used as modal verbs in a positive **statement**, there must be a word of negative meaning in the same clause. This word can be outside the verb phrase and may be a word with a negative sense, such as *only*, *never*, *hardly*.

> He **need only** ask and I will tell him.
> **No** sensible driver **dare** risk that chance.

As a modal verb, **dare** has forms as follows:

I **dare** not **go**.	I **dared** not **go**.
He **dare** not **go**.	He **dared** not **go**.

> **Dare** I **do** it?
> **Dare** he **do** it?
> **Daren't** he **do** it?

As a main verb, **dare** has forms as follows:

I **dare to do** it.	I **do** not **dare to do** it.
He **dares to do** it.	He **did** not **dare to do** it.
He **does** not **dare to do** it.	**Does** he **dare to do** it?
He **doesn't dare to do** it.	**Doesn't** he **dare to do** it?

As a modal verb, **need** has forms as follows:

I **need** not **go**.	**Need** I **go**?
He **need** not **go**.	**Need** he **go**?
He **needn't** go.	**Needn't** he **go**?

As a main verb, **need** has forms as follows:

I **need** it.	I **need to do** it.
He **needs** it.	He **needs to do** it.
I **do** not **need to go**.	I **do** not **need to do** it.
He **does** not **need to go**.	**Does** he **need to go**?

- Either of the two forms of *dare* and *need* can be used for sentences that have much the same meaning.

  > Anna **didn't dare to jump** off the high fence.
  > Anna **dared not jump** off the high fence.
  > You **don't need to come** if you don't want to.
  > You **needn't come** if you don't want to.

Used to

The verb **used to** is a 'marginal' modal verb. Unlike the other modal verbs, it is only found in the past tense. Therefore, when it is used with **do** to make negatives and questions, the form of the auxiliary verb is always **did**.

Used to is used as follows:

– to describe an activity or a state that happened many times in the past.

> Gerry always **used to** go for a run before breakfast.
> Peter **didn't use to** say things like that when I knew him.

– to refer to an activity or state that was true in the past but is no longer true.

> I **used to** like rock climbing when I was younger.
> You **didn't use to** be so stressed!

Used to takes the following forms:

– The form **used to** is used with all subjects e.g. I, we, you, he, she, it, they.

I **used to**	We **used to**
You **used to**	You **used to**
She **used to**	They **used to**

> I **used to** live in New Zealand.
> He **used to** deliver newspapers papers but he owns the shop now.
> Nancy and Bill **used to** live in California.

There are two forms for a negative:

– **did not/didn't use to**.

> We **didn't use to** have central heating when I was a child.
> Alan **didn't use to** like children, but it's different now he has
>   his own.

– **used not/usedn't to**.

> I **used not to** be able to watch myself on TV at all.
> We **used not to** worry much about money.
> Things **usedn't to** be so bad.

There are two forms for a question:

– **did** + **subject** + **use to** + **base form**:
  e.g. **did he use to**...?

> **Did** they **use to** visit you often? – Well, Mary **used to**.

– **used** + **subject** + **to** + **base form**:
  e.g. **used he to**... ?

> **Used he to** play the guitar?

• In negatives, the form with *did* is used the most. In questions,
  the form with *did* is almost always preferred.

The common contracted negative form is **didn't use to**. The rarer
contracted negative form is **usedn't to**.

Do not confuse *used to* + **base form** with *be used to*
+ **present participle**, where *used to* means *accustomed to*.

> They lived in India for a long time, so they **are used
> to eating** spicy food.

Phrasal verbs

A **phrasal verb** is a type of verb that is created when a main verb is combined with either:

- an **adverb**,

    take off   *give in*
    blow up   *break in*

- a **preposition**,

    get at (*someone*)   ***pick on*** (*weaker children*)

- or an **adverb** + **preposition**,

    put up with (*insults*)   ***get out of*** (*doing something*)

Type A. Verb plus adverb

Some Type A phrasal verbs have no object, i.e. they are **intransitive**. The sentence makes sense without any further addition to the verb.

    *Mary **went away**.*
    *Helen **sat down**.*
    *The students **came back**.*

Others do require an object, i.e. they are **transitive**.

    *We could **make out** a figure in the distance.*
    *He tried to **blow up** the Houses of Parliament.*
    *Could you **put** your clothes **away**, please?*

If the object is a **noun**, many Type A phrasal verbs will allow the adverb to come either:

- before the object,

> I **picked up** Jim on my way home.
> He **blew out** the candle.
> She **tidied away** her things.

- or after the object.

> I picked **Jim up** on my way home.
> He blew **the candle out**.
> She tidied **her things away**.

If the object is a **pronoun**, it must come before the adverb.

> I picked **him up**.
> He blew **it out**.
> She tidied **them away**.

Sometimes you can guess the meaning of these verbs from the meanings of the parts.

> to **sit down** = sit + down
> to **go away** = go + away

Sometimes you have to learn the new meanings, or use a dictionary.

> to **make up** (an answer)   = invent
> to **turn down** (an invitation) = decline
> to **work out** (a problem)   = solve
> to **put up** (a visitor)   = accommodate

Type B. Verb plus preposition

Type B phrasal verbs always have an object. This is because prepositions always have an object.

> He **asked for** his bill.
> He **asked for** it.
> She **listened to** the doctor.
> She **listened to** her.
> They **referred to** our conversation.
> They **referred to** it.

Sometimes there are two objects – the object of the verb and the object of the preposition.

> He **asked** the waiter **for** the bill.

Type C. Verb plus adverb and preposition

Type C phrasal verbs are a combination of the two previous kinds of verb. All the parts of a Type C phrasal verb come before the object.

> We are **looking forward to** our holiday/it.
> Don't **put up with** bad behaviour/it.
> You must **look out for** the warning signs/them.

- It is sometimes hard to tell adverbs and prepositions apart, because often the same word can be both a preposition and an adverb, depending on how it is used. For further information about prepositions see p. 219.

The following are examples of the three types of phrasal verb that are explained on p. 81.

Type A

Phrasal verbs made from a verb plus an adverb may be intransitive (do not take an object) or transitive (take an object).

some phrasal verbs that do not take an object	*some phrasal verbs that do take an object*
to break down	to blow something up
to carry on	to break something off
to fall down	to bring a child up
to get about	to bring a subject up
to get up	to catch somebody up
to give up	to clear something up
to go away	to close something down
to go off	to give something up
to go on	to leave something out
to grow up	to make something up
to hold on	to pick someone up

Type B

Phrasal verbs made from a verb plus a preposition are all transitive.

to add to something	to hope for something
to agree with someone	to insist on something
to apply for a job	to laugh at something
to approve of something	to listen to something
to arrive at a place	to look after someone
to ask for something	to look for something
to believe in something	to look into something
to belong to someone	to pay for something
to call on someone	to refer to something
to care for someone	to rely on someone
to come across something	to run into someone
to deal with something	to run over something

Some Type B verbs are doubly transitive, since both the verb and the preposition can have an object.

to **add** insult **to** injury
to **ask** a grown-up **for** help
to **check** your answers **with** the teacher
to **pay** the assistant **for** your shopping
to **refer** a customer **to** the manager

Type C

Phrasal verbs with an adverb plus a preposition all take a prepositional object.

to be fed up with something	to keep away from something
to carry on with something	to look back on something
to catch up with something	to look forward to something
to check up on something	to look out for something
to come up with something	to look up to someone
to cut down on something	to make up for something
to do away with something	to put in for something
to face up to something	to run away with something
to fall back on something	to run out of something
to get on with someone	to run up against something
to get out of something	to stand up for something
to go back on something	to walk out on someone
to go in for something	to watch out for something
to break in on someone	to lead up to something

Tense

Time reference

Verb forms help us make time reference through their **tense**. Tense shows whether an action or a state took place in the past or takes place in the present.

> Jessica **works** in the post office.
> Laurence **worked** in the post office over the Christmas holidays.

There are two **simple tenses** and six **compound tenses**.

Simple tenses

The simple tenses consist of a single word.

There is a **present simple** tense

I **like**	I **live**
you **like**	you **live**
he **likes**	he **lives**

and a **past simple** tense.

I **liked**	I **lived**
you **liked**	you **lived**
he **liked**	he **lived**

The simple tenses of regular verbs

The **present tense** is the same as the **base form** of the verb, except that an **-s** is added to the verb when it has a noun or *he, she,* or *it* as a subject. This is called the 3rd person singular form.

> *he/she/it* like**s**
> *he/she/it* live**s**

The **past tense** of a regular verb is made from the **base form** of the verb with **-ed** (or **-d** if the verb already ends in **-e**) added. The spelling is the same for all persons.

> *I* **liked**   *I* **lived**
> *you* **liked**   *you* **lived**
> *he* **liked**   *he* **lived**

The simple tenses of irregular verbs

Most irregular verbs make the **present tense** from the **base form** of the verb just as regular verbs do.

> Present
> *I* **find**   *I* **go**
> *you* **find**   *you* **go**
> *he/she/it* **finds**   *he/she/it* **goes**

- Irregular verbs make the **past tense** in a number of different ways. Sometimes the past tense is a completely different word. See pp. 32–34 for more on irregular verbs.

> Past
> *I* **found**   *I* **went**
> *you* **found**   *you* **went**
> *he/she/it* **found**   *he/she/it* **went**

Aspect

When we use a verb, we often need to be able to refer to more than the time at which an event took place. We sometimes need to be able to refer to actions and states as completed or not completed. **Aspect** describes the way we think of verbal actions.

The **continuous aspect** is formed by using the appropriate form of the auxiliary *be* together with the *-ing* form (**present participle**) of the main verb.

We use **continuous aspect** to show that an action:

– is going on at the time of speaking.

> *I'm having dinner at the moment. Can I call you back?*
> *I know what you are doing!*
> *Look! Someone's walking around in our garden!*

– was going on throughout the time that you are referring to.

> *I was having dinner when he called.*
> *I was waiting for her when she came out of the classroom.*
> *We were driving home when we saw the accident.*

– will be going on at the time that you are referring to.

> *We're going to Turkey for a holiday next year.*
> *They're coming to us for Christmas this year.*

The **perfect aspect** is formed by using the appropriate form of the auxiliary *have* together with the *-ed* form (**past participle**) of the main verb.

We use **perfect aspect** to show that an action:

– is complete at the time of speaking.

> I**'ve finished** the book. It was brilliant.
> We**'ve enjoyed** having you all to stay.
> Jo **has borrowed** the book, so I can't check now, I'm afraid.

– was complete at the time you are referring to.

> Oh dear; I **had forgotten** my promise to Aunt Jane.
> Sharon **had lost** her key, so she had to wait outside.
> Sue **had seen** the film three times already, but she didn't mind.

It is possible to have a compound tense that shows both aspects, continuous and perfect.

> Peter **has been talking** about you a lot recently.

Compound tenses

The compound tenses are a combination of present or past **tense** (shown through an auxiliary verb) with continuous or perfect **aspect**. See also pp. 88–89.

> I'm **doing** my homework at the moment, so I can't come out.
> Ben **has seen** the camera that he wants.

> She **was listening** to the radio in the kitchen.
> Sandra **had invited** all her friends.

- The tense of the auxiliary verb shows whether the compound verb is **present** tense,

> I'm **having** dinner at the moment; I'll call you back.
> We'**ve had** a lovely stay; thank you.

or **past** tense.

> We **were dancing** around the living room and singing along.
> Mum **had gone out** and left us some snacks.

The choice of the **auxiliary** and the **participle** shows what aspect the verb has.

- if it is the auxiliary **be** and the **-ing** participle (the present participle), the aspect is **continuous**.

> My brother **is having** a party tomorrow.
> The kids **were running** wild when we got home.

- if it is the auxiliary **have** and the **-ed** participle (the past participle), the aspect is **perfect**.

*Jill **has walked** more than 500 miles for charity.*
*Someone **had tied up** the dog to stop it wandering off.*

These are the main compound tenses:

present continuous   = present of **be** + **-ing** participle.

*Kerry **is waiting** until Jessica gets here.*

past continuous   = past of **be** + **-ing** participle.

*Maria **was watching** TV when Jo called.*

present perfect   = present of **have** + **-ed** participle.

*Sam **has seen** a few things that he'd like.*
*We**'ve bought** some better equipment.*

past perfect   = past of **have** + **-ed** participle.

*She **had** really **believed** their story!*
*Rory **had had** enough of their silly questions.*

A compound verb can also combine both the continuous and perfect aspects, using **two auxiliary verbs** and a **main verb**. This produces the following combinations:

present perfect continuous
   = present of **have** + past participle of **be** + **-ing** participle.

*For the past two months, Zoe **has been visiting** us once a week.*
*We**'ve been trying** to finish that job since Easter.*

past perfect continuous
= past of **have** + past participle of **be** + **-ing** participle.

> Vicky **had been hoping** for better news.
> I **had been travelling all day**, so I was exhausted.

The modal auxiliaries can be used in compound tenses.

> She **might be babysitting** for us on Friday.
> We **would be sitting** here for hours if I told you everything.
> I **may have eaten** something that disagreed with me.
> I expect Nayeema **will have bought** something for tea.

They come in first position in the verb phrase, so they are followed by:

- the subject and the rest of the verb in questions.

> **Will you be going** shopping after work?

- the negative **not** and the rest of the verb in negative statements.

> Marcus **may not have been** entirely truthful.

- the subject, the negative **not**, and the rest of the verb in negative questions.

> **Will you not be pushing** for that to be changed?

If the contracted negative form of the modal is used, then it comes before the subject and and the rest of the verb.

> **Won't** he **be calling** on us this evening?

Modals are not used with the supporting auxiliary verb **do**.

See pp. 58–80 for the meanings and uses of modal auxiliary verbs.

Responses

You usually use just the first part of the verb phrase in a compound verb as the response form. That is, you use one of the auxiliary verbs. If it is a simple tense you use the supporting auxiliary *do*.

> **Do** you **like** avocados? – Yes, I **do**.

If one of the forms of *be* or **have** is the first verb in the verb phrase, then use that as the response form.

> **Has** Claire been round yet? – Yes, she **has**.
> **Was** Nayeema asking for help? – Yes, she **was**.

If a **modal** verb is first in the verb phrase, some speakers prefer to use the modal and the auxiliary form together as the response form.

> Do you think he **might have left** the parcel somewhere? –
>   Yes, he **might** or Yes, he **might have**.
> So Laurence **could be coming** with us then. – Yes, he **could**
>   or Yes, he **could be**.

The present simple tense

Typical forms of this tense are as in:

> *I know her.*
> *He knows her.*

The present simple tense of *do* is used as the supporting auxiliary when you want to:

- ask a question,

> ***Do** I know you?*
> ***Does** she know you?*

- make a negative statement using **not**,

> *I **do not** know her.*
> *She **does not** know you.*

- or give a short response.

> ***Do** you just **have** coffee for breakfast? – Yes, I **do**.*

We use the present simple tense to talk about:

- habits, likes and dislikes, and things that happen regularly.

> *I **like** coffee for breakfast but everyone else in my family*
>   ***prefers** tea.*
> *I **don't take** sugar in my coffee.*
> *What **does** Jamie **usually have** for breakfast?*
> *They **often go** to the cinema **on Saturdays**.*
> *I **don't usually watch** TV.*

(When we talk about habits, we often add adverbs such as *often*, *always*, *usually*, *sometimes*, or *never*, or adverbial phrases such as *on Sundays* or *in the summer*.)

– statements of fact that are scientific truths or that are about a permanent state.

> The sun **rises** in the east.
> Birds **fly** south in the winter.
> We **live** in Scotland.

– statements that indicate the speaker's opinions or beliefs.

> I **think** he's a very good teacher.
> I **don't agree** with that at all.

– for dramatic narrative to tell a story or describe an action vividly,

> He **walks** slowly to the checkout and **puts** his bag on the counter. As the cashier **opens** the till he **draws** a gun ...

– or when giving a commentary on a sports event or public function.

> ... but Nadal **sees** it. He **runs** up to the net and **smashes** the ball.

We can also use the present simple for planned future actions with a time adverb, for example to talk about travel plans and timetables. See pp. 110–117 for more about future reference.

> The train **leaves** at 10.40 a.m. and **arrives** at 3.30 p.m.

We use the present simple in conditional sentences about real possibilities that affect the future. See p. 273 for more on conditional sentences.

> If I **lend** you my notes, I won't be able to revise tonight.

The past simple tense

Typical forms of this tense are as in:

> I **met** her.
> She **met** him.
> I **went** there.
> She **went** there.

Because the past simple consists of one word only, the past simple tense of **do**, which is **did**, is used as the supporting auxiliary when you want to:

– ask a question,

> **Did** I **meet** him?
> **Did** she **meet** him?
> **Did** I **go** there?
> **Did** it **go** there?

– make a negative statement using **not**,

> I **did** not **meet** her.
> He **did** not **meet** her.
> I **did** not **go** there.
> He **did** not **go** there.

– or make a response.

> Did you see Jenny yesterday? – No, I **didn't**.
> Did Penny phone you? – Yes, she **did**.

We use the past simple tense to talk about:

– single actions in the past.

> He **locked** the door and **left** the house.
> I **went** out and **brought** the cat back in again.

– habitual actions in the past, often with *always*, *never*, or *often*.

> In those days I **always went** to Juliano's for lunch.
> I **cycled** in **every day** and that soon **made** me fit.
> I **often visited** Glasgow on business when I was in publishing.

– past actions where a definite time is mentioned. It is often used with a time expression such as *ago* or *last month*, when the action is seen as finished.

> **Some time ago** now, I **went** to America for a month.
> **Once upon a time** there was a king in a faraway land.
> I **saw** Roger **a little while back**.
> I **bought** the microwave **a year ago**.

– points where the main action is broken. The rest of the sentence uses the past continuous tense to describe the past activity or action.

> I was clearing out the garage when a car **came** down the drive.
> We were leaving the house when the phone **rang**.

The present continuous tense

Typical forms of this tense are as in:

> *I am winning.*
> *He is winning.*

> *Am I winning?*
> *Is she winning?*

> *I am not winning.*
> *He is not winning.*

> *Aren't I winning?*
> *Isn't she winning?*

> *Am I not winning?*
> *Is she not winning?*

Some main verbs are not normally used in the continuous in standard British English, though they may be used this way in other varieties of English. These are generally verbs about states rather than actions.

> *I am winning.*   **but not** *I am liking it.*
> *I am not winning.*   **but not** *I am not liking it.*

We use the present continuous tense to talk about:

– things that are happening now, at the time when we are talking.

> *Mum**'s mowing** the lawn, and I**'m doing** my homework,*
>   *but Isabel **isn't doing** anything.*
> *The children aren't asleep; they**'re messing about**.*
> *Come on; you**'re not trying**.*

When you give a short answer to a question, it is normal to echo the auxiliary but not the main verb.

> **Are** you **waiting** for someone? – Yes, I **am**.
> **Is** Hamish **working** in the library? – No, he **isn't**.

– a temporary activity, even if it is not happening at the time when we are talking.

> I**'m studying** German at college.
> I**'m thinking** of getting a new car.

– a temporary situation in contrast to a permanent situation.

> I**'m living** in Scotland **at the moment**.
> Fiona **is working** in the stables over the holidays.

– a changing state or situation.

> My headache **is getting** better.
> The daylight **is slowly fading**.

– the circumstances under which something is generally done.

> I have to wear glasses **when I'm driving**.

– arrangements for future events along with a time adverb or phrase. See p. 110 for more on the future.

> I **am flying** to New York **next week**.

We also use it to express annoyance at a repeated action. In this case, one of the following adverbs is used with the verb: *always, forever, constantly, continually*.

> She**'s always whining** about something.
> He**'s forever** laughing and making silly comments.

The past continuous tense

Typical forms of this tense are as shown in:

> *I was winning.*   **but not** *I was liking it.*
> *She was winning.*
> *They were winning.*

> *Was I winning?*
> *Was she winning?*
> *Were you winning?*

> *I was not winning*   **but not** *I was not liking it.*
> *We were not winning.*
> *They weren't winning.*

Some main verbs are not normally used in the continuous in standard British English, though they may be used this way in other varieties of English. These are generally verbs about states rather than feelings.

We use the past continuous tense in these ways:

– with a time expression, such as *at 6p.m. yesterday*, to talk about an action that began before that time and finished after it. The exact length of time the action took is not important.

> *What **were you doing** at eight o'clock last night? –*
> *I **was standing** at the bus stop.*

– to talk about an interrupted action. Note that for the event that interrupts the action, we use the past simple tense.

> *We **were** all **sitting** in our places when the bell **rang**.*

– to talk about a longer action that was already taking place when a short action happened.

*While I **was waiting** for the bus I **dropped** my purse.*

– to describe a scene in the past, especially in a story.

*It was a dreadful morning. The snow **was still falling**, the wind **was blowing**, and the cars **were skidding** on the icy roads.*

The present perfect tense

Typical forms of this tense are as shown in:

> I **have finished**.
> He **has found** them.
> They**'ve finished**.
> They**'ve found** her.
> Listen! **I've heard** some great news; Jim**'s won**!
> They**'ve bought** a brand new car.
> You**'ve got** a nerve!

> **Have** they **finished**? – No, they **haven't**.
> **Has** Mary **arrived** yet? – No, she **hasn't**.

> I **have** not **finished**.
> He **has** not **finished**.
> Ranee **hasn't found** her bracelet yet.
> They **haven't seen** her.

The contracted forms are:

has = **'s**   have = **'ve**
has not = **hasn't**   have not = **haven't**

The present perfect tense is used to talk about events that are relevant to the present but that happened in the past. It is used to talk about an action that started in the past, without mentioning a specific time.

> Her daughter **has had** an accident.
> We **have seen** the Eiffel Tower and the Arc de Triomphe.

If the present perfect occurs more than once in a compound sentence, the second and subsequent instances of **have** can be left out.

> They **have bought** their tickets and **booked** their seats.

- We can use *just* if we want to show that the action has very recently been completed.

  > They **have just bought** their tickets.
  > He **has just finished** his homework.

  If the event did not take place you can use *never*. If you want to find out whether it took place or not, you can use *ever*.

  > **Have** you **ever been** to Greece?
  > I**'ve never done** anything like this before.

- If we want to indicate a moment in time or a period of time, we can use expressions such as *recently*, *lately*, *this morning*, *today*, or *this week* with the present perfect tense.

  > I **haven't been** to the cinema **recently**.
  > I**'ve waited a week** for your answer.

- In questions and negative sentences, the present perfect can be used with *yet*, meaning 'at the time of speaking'. In positive sentences, use *already*.

  > **Haven't** you **finished yet**?
  > **Have** you **bought** the tickets **yet**?
  > I**'ve** already **seen** that film.

The present perfect tense is often used to answer the question *How long...?* together with *for* to talk about a period of time, or *since* to talk about duration from a point in time.

  > I **have lived** in Edinburgh **for** fifteen years.
  > **How long have you lived** in Edinburgh?
  > We**'ve had** this car **since** 2008.
  > We **haven't spoken** to each other **since** the night of the argument.

The past perfect tense

Typical forms of this tense are as shown in:

> I **had misheard**.
> She **had misheard**.
> I **had finished**.
> She **had found** them.
> She**'d gone**.
> They**'d found** her.

> **Had** I **misheard**?
> **Had** it **gone**?
> **Had** Mary **arrived** before Peter told you? – No, she **hadn't**.

> I **had** not **misheard**.
> He **had misheard**.
> I **had** not **finished**.
> It **had** not **worked**.
> I **hadn't realized** how serious the problem was.
> They **hadn't seen** her.

The contracted forms are:

> had = **'d**   had not = **hadn't**

The past perfect tense goes one step further back into the past than the present perfect.

> **Had** you ever **seen** her before then? – No, I **hadn't**.

The past perfect tense is used to talk about:

– an action that took place in the past before something else took place.

> She **had just made** some coffee when I arrived.

– an action or state that began before another action in the past and continued up to the time of the second action and perhaps even beyond that time.

> Ashraf **had** already **known** my brother **for two years** when
>   I met him.

• It is often used in the main clause of a complex sentence, to set the scene for a past event.

> We **had always wanted** to visit Canada **for a long time**, so last
>   year we decided to go.

• It is often used with a time expression such as *always* or *for several days*.

> We **had always wanted** to visit Canada, so last year we decided
>   to go.

The present perfect continuous tense

Typical forms of this tense are as shown in:

> I **have been waiting**.
> I'**ve been waiting**.
> She **has been waiting**.
> She'**s been waiting**.

> **Have** I **been snoring**?
> **Has** he **been waiting**?
> **Have** you **been waiting** long?

> I **have** not **been waiting**.
> She **has** not **been waiting**.

We use the present perfect continuous tense to talk about:

– actions and states that began in the past and are still continuing at the time of speaking.

> I **have been holding** this ladder for ages. When are you going to come down?

– actions and states that began in the past and have only just finished.

> Thank goodness you're here! I'**ve been waiting** for hours.

– repeated actions.

> I'**ve been getting** this magazine every week for a year.

There is sometimes little difference between the meaning of the present perfect and the meaning of the present perfect continuous when they are used for long-term actions.

> **I have been working** here for three years.
> **I have worked** here for three years.

We usually choose the continuous form for more temporary actions or states.

> **I have been living** in London since I left school.

... and the present perfect form for more permanent ones.

> **I have lived** in London since I was born.

- We cannot use this tense with verbs such as *be*, *know*, and *like*, which are not used in continuous forms.

- We can use *for* and *since* with the continuous form in the same way as with the present perfect form. See also pp. 98–101 for more about continuous uses of the verb.

> **I have been studying** English for three years.
> **I have studied** English for three years.

> **I have been living** in London since I left school.
> **I have lived** in London since I was born.

The past perfect continuous tense

Typical forms of this tense are as shown in:

> I **had been waiting**.
> I'**d been waiting**.
> She **had been waiting**.
> She'**d been waiting**.

> **Had I been talking nonsense**? *What had I said?*
> **Had he been waiting** *long?*
> **Had you been expecting** *to meet Mary at the station?*

> I **had not been waiting**.
> She **had not been waiting**.
> They **hadn't been looking** *very carefully.*

The past perfect continuous tense is used to talk about an action which began before another action in the past and either:

– continued up to the time of the second action,

> I **hadn't been waiting** *long when a lorry drew up beside me.*

– or was completed before the second action happened.

> I **had been studying** *and decided to take a stroll to clear my mind.*
> We **had been cleaning** *the car for hours, so we stopped and had a drink.*

• The past perfect continuous is often used in the main clause of a complex sentence, to set the scene for an event.

> I **had been driving** *for about an hour when I* **heard** *a noise in the engine.*

- The past perfect continuous is often used to talk about a repeated action.

  *She **had been trying** to telephone her mother all day.*

  Remember that you cannot use the past perfect continuous with verbs such as *like*, which are not used in the continuous. See p. 98.

Future reference

Verb forms

English has no future tense as such. However, several forms, especially the **modal** verbs *will* and *shall*, can be used to make future reference. These forms are summarized as follows:

1 *Will/shall* + the **base form** makes the most direct form of future reference. See p. 66. The other modal verbs that express possibility make a more indirect reference to future time.

> *It **will take** several years to finish.*
> *Jean **will look after** the dogs while we're away.*
> *I **shall** simply **tell** her to mind her own business.*
> *We **shall see**.*

2 *Be going to* + the **base form** is used to express intention and make predictions. See p. 113.

> *He failed his exam last year; this year he **is going to work** harder.*
> *You'd better take the washing in; it **is going to rain**.*

3 The **present continuous tense** is used to talk about plans and arrangements in the future with a time adverb. See p. 98.

> *Sarah and Harriet **are meeting at ten o'clock** on **Tuesday**.*
> *I **am flying** to Glasgow **on Friday**.*

4 The **present simple tense** is used with a time adverb to talk about future plans which are part of a timetable or previous arrangement. See p. 94.

> *The main film **starts at 2.45 p.m.***
> *We **leave at 4 p.m. tomorrow**.*

5 The **future perfect tense** (*will have* + the **past participle**) is used with a time adverb to talk about an action that will be finished at the time in the future that you are referring to. See p. 115.

> *I was hoping to meet James, but by the time I arrive he **will have gone** home.*

6 *Be about to* + the **base form** is used to talk about the very near future. See p. 116.

> *I'm sorry I can't stop and chat; I**'m about to leave** for work.*

7 The **future continuous tense** (*will be* + the **present participle**) is used to talk about future action in progress. See p. 117.

> *What **will** you **be doing** on Saturday morning? Oh, I'll **be shopping** as usual.*

8 *Be to* + the **base form** is used to talk about formal plans, especially in journalism. See p. 117.

> *The President **is to attend** an EU–Russia summit tomorrow.*

1 **will/shall**
The modal verbs *will* or *shall* followed by the **base form** of a main verb are used to express future reference.

I **shall come**.	We **shall come**.
or	or
I **will come**.	We **will come**.
You **will come**.	You **will come**.
She/he/it **will come**.	They **will come**.

Will can be used with all persons of the verb, although some speakers prefer to use *shall* in the 1st person singular and plural. See p. 66 for further details.

- The contracted form is **'ll** for both verbs, so there is no difference in informal speech.

    I'll probably be late, but I expect they'll be on time.

    The contracted negative forms are **won't** and **shan't**.

    We won't come.
    We shan't come.

- If there are two verbs in the sentence, it is normal not to repeat the modal form before the second one.

    I won't see him or speak to him for six months.

We use **will** (or **shall**) for future reference in the following ways:

- to talk about future facts.

    I shan't see Mary next week.
    I'll be on the plane this time tomorrow.

- to make promises or reassurances.

    I'll be home in time for tea.
    This won't happen again, I can assure you.

- to announce a decision that the speaker has just made.

    Er, I'll have the pizza Margherita and a side salad, please.
    Right, I shall ask him, and see if his story matches yours.

- to express negative intention, using **won't**.

    I won't go there again. The service was dreadful.

– to express refusal.

> I **won't put up with** any more of this silly behaviour.
> I've tried to persuade her but she **won't come**.

– to talk about an event in the future, possibly in the distant future. A time clause may be used.

> People **will be** amazed when they hear about this in years to come.

– to refer to inevitable actions or events that will take place in the future.

> Christmas is past, but it **will come** again next year.

– to express an opinion about a future event after verbs such as *believe, expect, hope, know,* and *think.*

> I **expect** he**'ll be** home soon.
> I **hope** you**'ll be** very happy in your new home.

– to express a real possibility in conditional sentences. See p. 273.

> If you phone after six **I'll tell** you all about it.

2 **be going to**
Future reference can be made with *be* + *going to* + the **base form** of a main verb.

> I **am going to wait**.
> He **is going to wait**.
> I **am not going to wait**.
> He **is not going to wait**.
> **Is** he **going to wait**?
> **Are** they **going to wait**?

Be going to is used in the following ways:

- to express intention about the future.

    *Mary **isn't going** to study art; she**'s going** to be a nurse.*

- to talk about things that have already been decided.

    *Is Jim **going to leave** his job? – Yes, **he is**.*
    *Where's Mary? She said she **was going to come** early.*

- to make a prediction about the future, often the very near future, based on something in the present.

    *Watch the milk! It **is going to boil** over!*
    *Sally never does any work; she **is going to fail** her exams.*

If the past tense of **be** is used, a past intention or prediction can be expressed.

    *Judy **was going to meet** me, but she was ill and couldn't come.*
    *She **was** obviously **going to get** blisters with those new shoes.*

Note this difference:

Be going to is usually used for future events where the speaker expresses his or her intention.
Will is used to express decisions made at the moment of speaking.

    *I**'m going to go** to the pictures on Friday; would you like to come?*
    *Yes, I**'ll go** if Chris goes.*

3 Present continuous

The present continuous tense is used to talk about plans for the future, or specific arrangements that people have made for future events.

> The school **is having** a sale next week; I**'m running** the bookstall.

It is often used in questions about future arrangements.

> What **are you doing** on Saturday? – I**'m going** to a football match with Peter.
> When **are you leaving**? – At the end of term.

If there are two verbs in the sentence, it is normal not to repeat the auxiliary before the second and subsequent ones.

> We **are meeting** at 12.30 p.m., **having** a quick lunch, and **starting** work at 1.15.

4 Present simple

The present simple tense is also used to talk about events that form part of a timetable or programme.

> The train **leaves** Edinburgh at 10.10 a.m. and **arrives** in London at 3.20 p.m.
> These are the arrangements for Friday: doors **open** at 7 p.m., the Mayor **arrives** at 7.30 p.m., and the meeting **starts** at 7.45 p.m.

5 The future perfect (*will have* + the past participle of a main verb)

This form is used to talk about an action that will be complete at a time in the future that you are talking about. It is often used with verbs relating to finishing or completing.

The contracted positive form is **'ll have** or **will've**.

> *Can you come round next Saturday? – Yes,* I'll **have finished** *my exams by then.*
> *Dad* **will've made** *dinner by the time we get back.*

The contracted negative is **won't have**.

> *The essay is due on Tuesday, but* I **won't have completed** *it by then.*

In questions, the subject comes after **will**. The short answer to a question is **will** without the past participle.

> **Will** *you* **have finished** *dinner by then? – Yes,* **we will**.

6 *be* + *about to* + **the base form**

The appropriate form of **be** + **about to** + the **base form** of a main verb is used to talk about events in the very near future.

> *Turn off the gas – the soup* **is about to boil** *over.*
> *Come on! The film's* **about to start**!

It is sometimes used with **just** following the **be** word to give even more immediacy.

> *Quick, jump in! The train* **is (just) about to leave**.

Be about to can also be used in the **past** to suggest that someone is *on the point of* carrying out an action when it is interrupted. In this case it is usually followed by **when**.

> *They* **were (just) about to go** *to bed* **when** *the phone rang.*

7 **The future continuous tense**
This is made with **will** + **be** + the **present participle** of a main verb. **Will be** forms negatives, contractions, questions, and short answers in the usual way.

The future continuous is used in a rather informal way to suggest that something is about to happen or will happen at some time that is not clear or precise.

> I'**ll be seeing** you.
> We'**ll be getting** in touch with you.
> They'**ll be wanting** us to clean our own classrooms next!
> We **won't be seeing** Uncle John while we are in Australia.

It is also used to talk about an activity that will already be in progress at a particular time in the future.

> **Will** you **be working** here next week?
> No, I won't. I'**ll be starting** my new job.
> Just think! This time next week, we **will be flying** to Sydney.

8 **be to** + the base form
The appropriate form of **be** + **to** + the **base form** of a main verb is used mainly in fairly formal English to talk about plans, arrangements, and instructions. It indicates that what will happen is part of an expected process, and is often found in journalistic texts.

> Foreign ministers of the NATO countries **are to meet** in Brussels next week.
> The President has left for Geneva, where he **is to attend** the meeting.

Active and passive

Active sentences

In the following example, the verb is **active**.

> *The postman delivers hundreds of letters every day.*

The subject of an active sentence is also the person or thing that carries out the action. We use the active when the subject of the verb is the doer of the action. The active is used in most English speech and writing, because we usually want to inform our listener or our reader who or what carried out the action of the verb.

> *He hid the money under the bed.*
> *The car knocked over a pedestrian.*
> *I'm sending the book by express delivery.*

Passive sentences

In the following example, the verb is in the **passive**.

> *Thousands of letters are delivered every day.*

The subject in a passive sentence is not the person or thing that does the action of the verb. It is the person or thing that is acted on by the verb.

> *The injured man was helped by a passer-by.*
> *The man was being questioned by the police.*
> *The patient was operated on by a team of five surgeons.*

The passive is made with the appropriate form of *be* + the **past participle** of the main verb.

- We use the passive to direct our listener's attention to the important part of our message. For instance, in the first example of this section we do not need to know who delivers the letters, so all mention of the postman is left out.

- The passive can be used when we do not know who carries out the action expressed by the verb, or when it is not important that we should know. It is sometimes much more important to know what has happened than who or what did it.

> The money **was hidden** under the bed.
> The book **is being sent** by express delivery.
> An elderly man **was run over** while crossing the road.
> Roger **has been given** his promotion.
> The patient **was operated on**.

The passive allows us to select the parts of a sentence to which we want to draw attention. It can be used when we want to focus on:

- the **agent**, i.e. who brought the action about. We show the agent with *by*.

> The window was broken **by some boys**.
> My brother was given extra tuition **by his teacher**.
> The old man was run over **by a careless driver**.
> The patient was operated on **by a team of top surgeons**.

- the **instrument**, i.e. what was used to make the action happen. We show the instrument with *by* or *with*.

> The sorting is done **by machine**.
> The safe was blown open **with dynamite**.
> The old man was knocked over **by a bus**.
> I was showered **with presents** on my eighteenth birthday.

– the **means**, i.e. what caused the action to happen. We show the means with *by* or *with*.

> The window was shattered **by the explosion**.
> He was exhausted **with the strain of caring for his elderly parents**.
> Spelling errors are marked **with a cross in the margin**.
> He was taken to hospital **by ambulance**.

The subject of a passive verb

The verb in a passive sentence has the word that would normally be its object in the position of the subject. When a verb has two objects, either the indirect object or the direct object of the active verb may become the subject of the passive verb.

> **I've been offered** a place at university.
> **We were given** a second chance.

If the indirect object is mentioned after the passive verb, the sentence must use *to*.

> The building **has been sold to** property developers.
> The medal **is awarded to** students who have shown academic
>   excellence.

Some verbs that are often used this way are: *give, offer, lend, promise, sell,* and *tell*.

Form of the passive

Passive verbs are made from a form of *be* + the **past participle** of a main verb. In the passive, the form of the auxiliary verb *be* indicates the tense.

> They **sell** cheap computer games here.
> Cheap computer games **are sold** here.
> They **took** him to the police station for questioning.
> He **was taken** to the police station for questioning.

- Some verbs are only or mostly used in the passive, e.g. *be born* and *be deemed*.

> The film **was deemed** unsuitable for younger audiences.
> My brother and I **were born** in Wales.

The impersonal passive

This form of the passive sentence is useful when you want to report what is or was generally understood or accepted by a group of people.

> **The suitcase was found** to be empty.
> **The money is thought** to be missing.
> **The rumour is believed** to be true.

The form **it** + **passive** + **that** can be used when you do not want to mention the source of a report or rumour.

> **It is reported** that over a hundred people died in the explosion.
> **It is said** that his income is over £200 a minute.

The passive with *get*

In informal English, a type of passive is sometimes made with **get** instead of **be**.

> How did that teapot **get broken**?
> Our cat **got run over** last week.

Get is also used to form a small set of passive verbs in contexts which are not informal (or 'neutral'), e.g. *get dressed*, *get married*, *get lost*.

> Harriet **got lost** on the Underground.
> When are you two **getting married**?

The causative passive with *have*

There is another kind of verbal group that is like the passive, because the person who carries out the action of the main verb is not the person who is the subject of the clause. It expresses the idea that the subject caused or ordered someone to take the action mentioned.

> We **are having the garage door replaced**.
> She **had her hair cut short**.
> They **did not have the carpet cleaned** after all.

It has the form: ***have*** + **direct object** + **past participle**.

> Compare:
>
> *Ralph repaired his car* = Ralph did the work.
> *Ralph* **had** *his car* **repaired** = He paid someone else to do the work.

Finite and non-finite verbs

In a sentence, there is normally at least one verb that has both a **subject** and a **tense**. When a verb has a subject and a tense, it can be referred to as a **finite** verb.

> **We want** Charlie to act as club secretary.
> **I like** taking photographs of insects.
> Coming home last night, **I saw** a deer run across the road.

Some forms of a verb are referred to as **non-finite**. The **present** and **past participles** and the **to infinitive** are the most common of these. The base form is often used in a non-finite way. Every verb can be used in a clause in either a **finite** or **non-finite** way.

- A verb is finite if it is found in a clause in combination with a subject and a tense.

  > **I walked** home.
  > **We saw** a deer.
  > **They appreciate** a little praise now and then.

- It is non-finite if it is used:

- without the verb having a tense.

  > **To open**, tear off the tab.
  > **Looking** around, he noticed a letter on the floor.
  > **Worn out** by the heat, they stopped for a drink.

- with no agreement between the subject (if there is one) and the verb.

  > **That plan failing**, he gave up.
  > **Our guests departed**, we felt a little depressed.

A compound verb is actually made up of one finite part, which is always the first auxiliary verb, while the remaining non-finite parts are the base form or the participles.

In the following examples the finite part of the verb phrase is in blue italic:

> I *may* **have been joking** when I *said* that.
> Helen *was* **running** around screaming.
> I *had* **been living** in a dream for months.
> Olivia *is* **coming** round at 6 o'clock this evening.

The present simple and past simple forms of a verb are always finite.

> I **sing**.
> We **tell** stories at night.
> Maya **laughed**.
> The shelter **collapsed**.

- A non-finite verb is sometimes used immediately after a finite verb.

> I **like to get up** early at the weekend.
> Harriet really **dislikes cleaning** the cooker.
> I certainly **wouldn't want to see** him again.
> We **persuaded** them **to join** us.

Often a noun or pronoun can come between the finite verb and the non-finite one. See p. 128 and p. 129 for more on this.

> We **want** Charlie **to act** as club secretary.
> She **wanted** him **to wash** his hands in the bathroom.
> I don't **like** you **cleaning** your boots over the sink.

- When the second verb is an *-ing* form coming after a noun or pronoun, there can be a difference in grammar between two similar sentences. Both sentences below are acceptable, although the first example might seem ambiguous to some people. In the second sentence, the *-ing* form is used as a verbal noun. See also p. 130.

  *She didn't like **him** cleaning his boots over the sink.*
  *She didn't like **his** cleaning his boots over the sink.*

The non-finite parts of the verb

Non-finite parts of a verb are those that do not indicate number, person or tense. The common non-finite forms are:

- the **base form**
- the **present participle** or -*ing* form
- the **past participle**
- the **to infinitive**

There are also other non-finite forms, such as:

- the **continuous to infinitive**: *to be teaching*
- the **perfect to infinitive**: *to have taught*
- the **passive to infinitive**: *to be taught*

The base form

As well as serving as the verb form on which most of the other parts of the verb are based, the **base form** is frequently used as a non-finite part of the verb. Because of this it is sometimes called the '*bare infinitive*' or the '*infinitive without to*'.

The **base form** is used as a **non-finite** part of the verb in these ways:

- after modal verbs.

  *You must **stop** at the kerb before you cross.*
  *He should **think** before he speaks.*

- after *let's* (suggestion) and *let* (permission) and *make* (compulsion).

  ***Let's invite** Annette round for dinner.*
  ***Let** the cat **go**!*
  ***Make** him **stop**!*
  ***Let** him **finish** what he was saying!*

– after *feel, hear, see, watch* + an object.

> I **heard** him **run** downstairs.
> Later we **saw** them **leave** the house.

– after a **to** infinitive to which it is joined by *and*.

> I want you to sit and **listen**.
> Just wait and **see**.

– after *would rather* and *had better*.

> I would rather **go** out, but I think we had better **stay** home and finish the painting.

Verbs of perception may be followed either by the **base form** or by the **-ing** form. There is often a change of sentence meaning.

These verbs include: *see, hear, feel, smell, listen to, watch*.

> We watched her **park** the car = we watched the whole event.
> We watched her **parking** the car = we may only have seen part of the event.
> I heard a cuckoo **call** = I heard just one call.
> We heard the birds **singing** = We heard part of the song of the birds.

The *to* infinitive

The **to** infinitive is used as follows:

– after an adjective of quality such as *small, tall, agreeable, pleasant, funny* that is used in combination with **too**.

> *The child was **too small to reach** the switch.*
> *The knife was **too blunt to cut** the string.*

or (**not**) + adjective of quality + **enough**.

> *The child was **not tall enough to reach** the switch.*
> *The knife was **not sharp enough to cut** the string.*
> *I was **stupid enough to go** walking in flip flops.*

– after adjectives of emotion such as: *angry, happy, glad, sad, sorry, surprised*, to express the reason for the emotion.

> *I'm **glad to see** you.*
> *I'm **sorry to hear** your news.*

– after a 'behaviour' adjective such as: *good, kind, nice, silly, wrong*, (sometimes + **of** + another **noun phrase**).

> *It was **good of you to come**, and **kind of Jane to have sent** those flowers.*
> *It was **silly to go** off like that.*
> *It was **kind of you to ring** me.*

– after a **WH-** word such as: *how, what, where, whether, which, who, whom*.

> *We have no idea **what to get** for Tim's birthday.*
> *I don't know **where to go**.*
> *I can't think **how to do it**.*
> *They were wondering **who to see** first.*

– after a noun phrase such as *a good idea*, *a good thing*, *a mistake* (sometimes + *for* + another **noun phrase**).

> It was **a mistake for Jim to buy** that motorbike.
> It was **a good idea to stop** here.

– after an adjective such as *easy*, *difficult*, *hard*, *impossible* + *for* + **noun phrase**.

> It has never been **easy for David to sit** exams.

– after a verb followed by *for*, e.g. *ask*, *wait* + *for* + **noun phrase**.

> They **are waiting** for us **to decide**.

• The **to** infinitive can be used to express purpose or necessity after a verb followed by a pronoun or a noun.

purpose: I brought *it* **to read** on the train = so that I could read it.
necessity: There is **work to do**! = work that must be done.

Sometimes the particle **to** can be used alone, provided the meaning is clear, for example in a short response, when the whole verb form is used in a previous sentence or clause.

> Did you **meet** Tina? No, I wanted **to**, but she was ill.
> Are you going to **visit** the museum? Yes, we hope **to**.

The *to* infinitive and the *-ing* form

The **to** infinitive and the **-ing** form (the present participle) can each be used after certain verbs.

Verbs followed by the **to** infinitive include: *agree, arrange, attempt, choose, decide, fail, hope, learn, manage, offer, plan, seem.*

> I **agreed to help** Shona with her homework.
> The driver **attempted to remove** the flat tyre.
> I **hope to see** you again at the next meeting.

Verbs followed by an **object** + the **to infinitive** include: *advise, allow, command, forbid, force, invite, order, persuade, remind, teach, tell.*

> Peter advised Ron **to call the police**.
> Esther reminded her teacher **to set some revision**.

Verbs that can be followed *either* directly by the **to infinitive** or by an **object** + the **to infinitive** include: *ask, expect, help, intend, like, love, hate, mean, prefer, want, wish.*

> I certainly intended **to go** to the party.
> We really expected **Sally to pass** the exam.

> Note this difference:
> I want **to have** a cat = It will be my cat.
> I want **her to have** a cat = It will be her cat.
> Dad likes **to wash** the car = Dad washes the car.
> Dad likes **John to wash** the car = John washes the car.

Verbs followed by the **-ing** form include: *avoid, be used to, delay, dislike, escape, finish, forgive, give up, go on, imagine.*

> I usually **avoid going** into town late at night.
> Miriam **hates peeling** potatoes.
> Have you **finished reading** that book yet?

- Some verbs may be followed either by the **to** infinitive or by the **-ing** form with little or no change in meaning. These verbs include: *begin, start, cease, continue, intend, like, love, hate, prefer.*

    > He began **to run** around shouting.
    > He began **running** around shouting.
    > She likes **to swim** in the sea.
    > She likes **swimming** in the sea.
    > I can't bear **to see** violence.
    > I can't bear **seeing** violence.

- Some verbs may be followed either by the **to** infinitive or by the **-ing** form but the meaning of the sentence changes depending on the form that is used. These verbs include: *try, forget, remember.*

    > I **remembered to switch** the lights off before we went out.
    > I **remember switching** the lights off before we went out.
    > She **tried to talk** to him, but his secretary wouldn't put the call through.
    > She **tried talking** to him, but he wouldn't listen.

Particularly after verbs such as *go* and *come*, the **to** infinitive is understood to express purpose.

> She has **gone to do** the shopping.
> They **came** here **to learn** English.

Use of the verb followed by the **-ing** form concentrates on what happens. The second verb is really the object of the first one. These verbs include: *remember, forget, try.*

> I definitely **remember switching the lights off** before we went out.
> She **tried talking to him**, but he wouldn't listen.

Some **set expressions** are followed by *-ing*. These include: *it's not worth*, and *it's no fun*.

> It's **no fun going** out alone.
> It's **no use phoning** him; he's gone away.
> It's **worth trying** one more time.

The noun phrase

A noun phrase is a word or group of words that can function as the
subject, the **object**, or the **complement** in a sentence.

> ***The manager*** *interviewed **all the applicants** on Tuesday.*
> ***Lydia*** *was **the successful applicant**.*

See pp. 18–19 and pp. 230–231 for more information about these
functions. A noun phrase must always contain a noun or a pronoun.

A noun phrase may consist of only one word. That word will be either
a noun or a pronoun.

> ***Mary*** *left late.*
> ***She*** *left late.*
> ***Cheese*** *is expensive.*
> ***It*** *is expensive.*

A noun phrase may consist of more than one word. One of these
words, a noun or a pronoun, is the **headword**. The other words
describe or modify the headword.

> *the tall **girl***
> *the very tall **girl***
> *a strikingly beautiful **girl***
> *the tall **girl** with green eyes*

Words that go before the headword are called **premodifiers**. A noun
can be premodified by:

– a determiner. See p. 160.

> ***the*** *girl*   ***that*** *boy*
> ***a*** *spider*   ***some*** *rice*

– one or more adjectives. See pp. 160–190.

>   **tall** *girls*
>   **tall dark** *girls*
>   **tall dark handsome** *men*

– a number, another noun, or the present participle or past participle of a verb.

>   **three** *days*
>   *the* **railway station** *buffet*
>   *an* **annoying** *habit*
>   *an* **overworked** *man*

Words that go after the headword are called **postmodifiers**. A noun can be postmodified by:

– a prepositional phrase (a noun phrase with a preposition in front of it).

>   *the person* **in the corner**
>   *the view* **across the valley**
>   *the house* **opposite the church**
>   *creatures* **under the sea**

– a subordinate clause (usually one beginning with *who*, *which* or *that*). See p. 264.

>   *All the women* **who had gathered there** *finally went away.*
>   *Milk* **that has been kept too long** *can go sour.*

– less commonly, certain adjectives. See p. 160.

>   *the princess* **royal**
>   *the president* **elect**

- Personal pronouns are only rarely premodified or postmodified. See p. 203.

  > **Silly** me.
  > **Poor old** you.

Types of noun

Nouns can be classified according to what they refer to.

● Nouns that are really names are called **proper nouns**. Proper nouns usually refer to a particular named person or thing.

They include:

– the names of specific people.

> Anna Dickinson John Lennon
> Lucy White Mrs Merton

– geographical items.

> Spain Mount Everest
> China England
> The Thames Paris
> Covent Garden Balcombe Road

– days of the week, months, and annual Church festivals.

> Thursday June
> Christmas Easter

– patented goods and trade names.

> Hoover Persil
> Jaguar Samsung

– newspaper and magazine titles.

> The Times Vogue
> The New Scientist Time Out

- shop, cinema and theatre names, buildings.

> *The Odeon*   *New Look*
> *The Royal Mews*   *Nationwide*

- titles (the polite or professional labels that we give to people).

> **Doctor** *Johnson*   **Sir** *George Hardie*
> **Professor** *James*   **President** *Hollande*

A person's title is usually placed before his or her name. Proper nouns and titles are always written with an initial capital letter.

- All the other nouns that refer to things or species are called **common nouns**.

> *I put the **tennis balls** in that **basket** there.*
> *My **brother** and **sister** visited my **mother**.*
> *The **anger** that John felt was overwhelming.*

Common nouns can be divided into the following groups, according to their meaning:

Abstract nouns. These refer to intangible items.

> *honesty*   *anger*
> *idea*   *time*
> *ugliness*   *behaviour*

Concrete nouns. These refer to tangible items.

> *pig*   *granite*
> *table*   *butcher*
> *brother*   *sugar*

A concrete noun may refer to a living thing (**animate** nouns) or a physical object (**inanimate** nouns).

Collective nouns. These refer to collections of people or animals.

> a **herd** of cows
> a **swarm** of bees

Nouns may also be classified according to the words with which they are used, that is:

– whether or not the noun gives us information about **singular** and **plural number**.

– the other words that can be used in the same noun phrase.

This gives us a useful distinction between **countable nouns** and **uncountable nouns**.

Countable nouns refer to things that we can count: *one cat, two cats, seventeen cats,* and so on. They have singular and plural forms, which are shown by the spelling. They must be used with a determiner if they are singular.

> **Dogs** *ran wild in the streets.*
> **The dog** *is loose again.*
> *Fetch* **a chair** *for Maddy, will you?*
> *We've bought* **six new chairs**.

Uncountable nouns refer to:

– things that are not normally thought of as countable.

> *John asked me for some* **advice**.
> *Anna gave us some more* **information** *about her* **work**.
> **Homework** *occupied much of Sonia's evening.*

– qualities or abstract ideas.

> Our **knowledge** of outer **space** is increasing daily.
> Trevor gave **evidence** at the trial.
> **Anger** is a normal human emotion.

Uncountable nouns do not usually have a plural form. They are followed by a singular verb. They are not normally used with the indefinite article. (You cannot talk about 'an advice' or 'a money'.) When it is necessary to think of an item as countable it has to be used with a **partitive noun**. See p. 141.

> He bought seven **sheets of** cardboard.
> Let me give you **a piece of** advice.

Some examples of the commonest uncountable nouns are: *advice, anger, beauty, behaviour, conduct, despair, evidence, furniture, happiness, homework, information, safety, knowledge, leisure, money, news, progress, research.*

- Verbal nouns (p. 158), which are formed from the present participle of verbs, can also be used as uncountable nouns.

> Why don't you try **walking** to work?
> Brian was told to stop **smoking**.
> The **ringing** in his ears continued.

> Note that nouns that are uncountable in English may be countable in other languages. See p. 142.

Mass nouns

These are nouns that refer to a substance that can be divided or measured but not counted, e.g. *sugar*, *water*. They do not usually have an indefinite article in front.

> **Meat** *is usually more expensive than* **cheese**.
> **Sugar** *is quite cheap.*

Mass nouns only take a plural in special cases. They can be counted when they refer to:

– a particular type or types of the substance.

> *There was a buffet of bread and rolls, cheese,* **cold meats**
>   *and tea or coffee.*
> *Ros brought out a tempting selection of* **French cheeses**.
> **The principal sugars** *are glucose, sucrose, and fructose.*

– a serving of the substance.

> **Two teas**, *please.*
> *He went up to the bar and ordered* **two lagers**.

• Mass nouns are often used together with a partitive noun.

> *There are only* **two pieces of furniture** *in the room.*
> *There are* **three portions of meat** *in this special pack.*
> **Five pints of lager**, *please.*

Partitive nouns

Partitive nouns are commonly followed by *of*. They are used when we need to talk about a part of a mass noun or when we need to count the quantity of something that is referred to by an uncountable noun or a mass noun, especially when it is necessary to talk about:

- measurements and quantities with mass nouns.

> three **pieces** of toast   a **slice** of cheese
> a **bit** of fluff   two **spoonfuls** of sugar

- individual items with uncountable nouns.

> *Two **pieces** of furniture needed major repairs.*
> *We needed several **lengths** of string.*

- a collection of countable nouns.

> *The road was blocked by a **flock** of sheep.*
> *He has a small **herd** of dairy cows.*
> *There was a **crowd** of football supporters on the bus.*
> *A **couple** of cats were fighting.*

> Many collective nouns can be used as partitive nouns.
> See p. 138.

Nouns that have both countable and uncountable uses

Most nouns are either countable nouns or uncountable nouns, as explained on p. 138. Some nouns, however, behave like countable nouns in some sentences and uncountable nouns in other sentences. They usually have different meanings depending on how they are used. For example *time, light, history, space, laugh,* and *grocery* have more than one meaning.

> *Time passed slowly.*
> *She did it four **times**.*
> ***Light** travels faster than sound.*
> *The **lights** in this room are too bright.*
> *The rocket was launched into **space**.*
> *There are plenty of empty **spaces** on the shelves.*

Some nouns that are countable nouns in other languages are used only as uncountable nouns in English, e.g. *information, advice.*

> *He received all the necessary **information**.*
> *I don't need your **help**.*

Some nouns are used only in the plural form, even when we are talking about one item, e.g. *trousers, clothes, jeans.* We can use a partitive noun with *of* when referring to a single item.

> *These **trousers** need cleaning.*
> *Put the **scissors** back when you have finished with them.*
> *I need **a pair of pliers**.*
> *Liz gathered up **a bundle of clothes**.*

Gender of nouns

In some languages, nouns have **gender**. This means that a noun causes other words such as adjectives to change their spelling according to certain rules. Grammatical gender has little to do with biological gender. English does not have **grammatical gender** for nouns.

On the other hand, the **biological gender** of the thing or person referred to does affect a few areas of English grammar.

> a cow... **she** or **it**   a bull... **he** or **it**
> a girl... **she**   a boy... **he**

Gender distinctions are relevant where personal pronouns (p. 203) and possessive determiners (p. 160) have to be decided on. These distinctions are only noticeable in **singular** nouns.

> **He** found **his book**.
> **He** had been looking for **it**.
> **She** found **her book**.
> **She** had been looking for **it**.

There are also special cases, such as the association of neuter gender with babies and small animals, or feminine gender with a vehicle.

> I just saw a **mouse**. **It** was running across the room.
> The **spider** was spinning **its web**.
> The **beetle** crawled into **its hole**.
> **The baby** threw down **its** rattle.
> I've got a new boat; **she's** a real beauty.

Nouns denoting male persons and animals are **masculine** in that they are used with the pronouns and possessive determiners he, him, his.

Nouns denoting female persons and animals are **feminine** in that they are used with the pronouns and possessive determiners she, her, hers.

Barry saw Linda. **He** *called out to* **her** *that* **he** *had found* **her** *book.*
Marcia saw Paul. **She** *called out to* **him** *that* **she** *had found* **his** *book.*
Madeleine saw Kim. **She** *said 'Hello' to* **her**.

The pronouns and possessive determiners used to refer to common or **neuter** nouns are: *it, its.*

> **The truth** *will emerge.* **It** *always does.*

Nouns denoting inanimate objects and abstract notions are also neuter.

* Some nouns denoting people have the same form for masculine and feminine. Nouns used for a group, e.g. *government* or *team*, have **common** or **neuter** gender, even when we know that the group is made up exclusively of male or female members.

  > *The* **government** *has changed* **its** *policy.*
  > *The* **team** *has won* **its** *first medal at a major championship.*

With some nouns of common gender it might be possible to specify the gender if we had sufficient information. But if we do not have this knowledge, the choice of pronoun or possessive determiner becomes a problem.

> *a driver...he/she*
> *the cook...he/she*
> *doctor...he/she*

As a way around this problem, in informal and spoken English, **their** is often used after a singular noun or an indefinite pronoun. See p. 202. Some people consider this grammatically unacceptable, but it is widely used to avoid repetitions of *his or her* or *him or her*.

> *Each* **student** *must apply to* **his or her** *tutor for an extension.*
> **Everyone** *must apply to* **their** *tutor for an extension.*
> **Someone** *has left* **their** *coat in my room.*

The specialized terms used to name male, female and neutered animals show a number of gender differences.

horse	mare	stallion	gelding
–	cow	bull	steer
sheep	ewe	ram	–

Gender differences are also shown in the nouns that indicate relationships.

parent	mother	father
child	daughter	son

- Many nouns denoting an occupation have no explicit gender.

engineer	doctor	programmer
mechanic	lawyer	driver

Some occupations and professions have a special feminine form for the noun.

> Call your bank **manager** today.
> Sue is **manageress** of a hairdressing salon.
> **Actors** from all over the UK attended the ceremony.
> Here in the studio to talk about her new book is **actress** Mary Farrell.

Many people prefer to avoid these forms, regarding the distinction as unnecessary.

> J.K. Rowling is a highly successful **author**.
> Judi Dench is one of our finest **actors**.
> Michelle Stewart has been promoted to Branch **Manager**.

The forms **authoress** and **poetess** are now considered patronising and are rarely used.

Some speakers prefer to use a different form of the word or an entirely different word in order to avoid a gender-marked noun.

the chair**man**   the chair**person**   the **chair**

If necessary, the gender of a common noun can be made clear by adding a descriptive term such as *woman* or *male/female*.

*Would you prefer to see **a woman doctor**?*
***Male staff** should use locker room B.*

If we are discussing a country from an emotional, economic, or political viewpoint we sometimes use feminine gender.

***Poland** has made steady progress restructuring **her** economy.*

Showing possession through nouns

Possession can be shown in two ways:

> *The **man** was mending his **car**.*
> *The **car** was being mended by a **man**.*

- by adding -**'s** to a singular noun, or an irregular plural noun that does not end in -**s**.

> *one dog*   *one boy*   *several children*
> *the **dog's** bones*   *the **boy's** books*   *the **children's** toys*

- by adding -**'** to a plural noun.

> *more than one dog*   *more than one boy*
> *the **dogs'** bones*   *the **boys'** books*

There is also the **of possessive** (a phrase with **of** followed by a noun).

> *the side **of the ship***   *the end **of the queue***

The **of possessive** is not just a different way of saying the same thing as the -**'s** possessive.

> *the **boy's** pencil*   **but not** *the pencil of the boy*

The -**'s** possessive is generally used only with nouns referring to animate items (e.g. people and animals) and in time phrases.

> *the **driver's** foot*   *the **dog's** nose*
> ***today's** newspaper*   *a **week's** holiday*

The **of** possessive is generally used with nouns referring to inanimate things (i.e. objects) and abstract ideas.

> the leg **of the table**   the arm **of the sofa**
> the wheel **of the car**   the foot **of the bed**
> the world **of ideas**   the power **of thought**

The function of the possessive form in English is to:

– show possession.

> the **boy's** books   the **dog's** blanket

– show a relationship, with a person either as the originator or the user of the thing named.

> her **parents'** consent   the **student's** letter
> a **women's** club   the **children's** park

– indicate that a place is where someone works or lives.

> a **grocer's**   the **butcher's**
> a **solicitor's**   my **aunt's**

– show that something is a part of a whole.

> the leg **of the table**   the **dog's** nose
> the wheel **of the car**   the **girl's** shoulder

– add a descriptive element which premodifies a noun. It is a type of determiner. See also p. 160.

> **writer's** cramp   A **Winter's** Tale

Rules for the formation of the possessive -**'s** (apostrophe -**s**) and -**s'** (-**s** apostrophe) are as follows:

– most singular nouns add an apostrophe + -**s**.

> a **girl's** ring   a **cat's** face

– most plural nouns add an apostrophe after the plural form -**s**.

> the **boys'** football   five young **girls'** faces

There are exceptions for the following:

– common nouns that end in -**s** in the singular. When these are made plural the choice of -**'s** or a simple apostrophe is optional.

> a cactus   the **cactus'** spines
>   the **cactus's** habitat

– plural nouns not ending in -**s**, for example those that that have a plural ending in -**en**. In this case, add an apostrophe + **s**.

> **children's**   **men's**

– proper nouns and common nouns that end in -**s**. These usually add -**'s** in the singular unless the final sound of the basic word is [-iz], in which case, a simple apostrophe is sufficient.

> Mrs **Evans's** car   Mr **Jones's** fence
> **Keats's** poetry   the **Bates's** cat
> I like **Dickens's** novels
> Peter **Bridges'** car

Compound nouns (see p. 151) put the **-'s** or the simple apostrophe at the end of the complete compound.

> *my mother-in-law* *my **mother-in-law's** car*
> *the runner-up*   *the **runner-up's** trophy*
> *the fire-fighters*   *the **fire-fighters'** efforts*

Noun phrases that are descriptive of someone's role or profession put the **-'s** on the headword of the phrase.

> ***a stock market analyst's** annual income*
> ***the senior hospital consultant's** weekly visit*

If they use an *of* construction the **-'s** or simple apostrophe usually goes on the last noun.

> ***the President of Austria's** official car*
> ***the director of marketing's** personal assistant*

Compound nouns

A compound noun is a noun that is formed from two or more words. The meaning of the whole compound is often different from the meaning of the two words on their own. Compound nouns are very common. The main noun is normally the last one.

tea**pot**	head**ache**
washing **machine**	driving **licence**
self-**control**	CD **burner**

Compound nouns are commonly formed from the following word combinations:

- noun + noun,
- verb + noun,
- adjective + noun,
- phrasal verb used as noun,
- particle + noun.

noun + noun:	**boyfriend**	**skinhead**
verb + noun:	**breakfast**	**grindstone**
adjective + noun:	**software**	**hardware**
phrasal verb:	**a break-in**	**a take-over**
particle + noun:	**onlooker**	**aftershave**

> The term **particle** is used for a word which could be either an adverb or a preposition.

Compound nouns can be written:

– as one word.

> bookcase   *wallpaper*
> *birdcage*   *snowflake*

– as two words.

> *post office*   *fire engine*
> *eye shadow*   *cough sweets*

– with a hyphen.

> *window-cleaner*   *air-conditioning*
> *lamp-post*   *tee-shirt*

Consult a dictionary to discover how the word is normally written.
There are often alternative forms to be found, for example, *drop down
menu*, *drop-down menu*, and *dropdown menu* are all currently acceptable
forms of the same compound noun.

Nouns as modifiers

The compound noun *girlfriend* names a special sort of *friend*. Nouns can
also be used as **modifiers** without forming a compound noun.

> a **concrete** slab   old **oak** beams
> a **car** mechanic   a **store** manager

A noun that is used as a modifier has the same function as an
adjective. The first noun usually makes the second one more specific,
but we do not think of it as part of a combination that forms a new
word. See p. 186 for more on modifiers.

Number in nouns

Singular number is used when the noun refers to one item.
Plural number is used when the noun refers to more than one item.

Countable nouns have both singular and plural forms.

Uncountable nouns and **mass nouns** do not normally have a plural form. See p. 136 for more on the types of noun.

The regular plural ending of an English noun is **-s**.

cat	cats

These are the exceptions to the normal pattern:

singular noun ending	*plural noun ending*
-s, -ss, -ch, -x, -zz focus princess church box buzz	**-es** focuses princesses churches boxes buzzes
-o hero piano potato	**-s** or **-es** heroes pianos potatoes
consonant + **y** baby hobby	**-ies** babies hobbies
vowel + **y** key ray	**-s** keys rays

singular noun ending	plural noun ending
-f hoof dwarf thief roof	**-s or -ves** hoofs or hooves dwarfs or dwarves thieves roofs
-fe knife life	**-ves** knives lives

Irregular plurals

Some nouns have two plural forms.

fish	fish or fishes

Some of them have the same form in the singular and plural.

a sheep	ten sheep
a deer	seven deer

A few change a vowel to form the plural.

man	men
woman	women
foot	feet
mouse	mice

Some nouns form the plural with **-en**.

child	children
ox	oxen

Since it is not possible to give more than a selection of the irregular forms, you should check in a dictionary if you are in doubt. If the dictionary does not show the plural form, then you can assume that it is regular.

Compound nouns normally form the plural by adding **-s** to the last word of the compound.

a games console	*three games consoles*
a bookcase	*two bookcases*
an Indian take-away	*two Indian take-aways*

There are a few exceptions:

A compound noun formed from a noun and an adverb makes the first word plural.

a passer-by	*several **passers-by***

Compound nouns with *woman* as the first word make both words plural.

a woman doctor	*several **women** doctors*
a woman driver	*most **women** drivers*

A compound word which ends in **-ful** normally adds **-s** after **-ful**, but there is an alternative form with the **-s** following the base noun.

a cupful	*three **cupfuls/cupsful***
a spoonful	*two **spoonfuls/spoonsful***

Plural nouns with singular reference

Some nouns referring to clothes and tools where two equal parts are joined together, e.g. *trousers*, *binoculars*, and *tongs*, are treated as being plural and are followed by a verb in the plural.

*My shorts **are** dirty.*
*The scissors **are** on the table.*

To talk about one of these items we can use the expression *a pair of...*

*John bought **a pair of jeans**.*

To talk about more than one we talk about however many *pairs of...*

*Martina bought **five pairs of tights**.*

- When they are used as ordinary numbers, words such as *dozen* and *million* have no plural form.

   nine million stars   **two dozen** glasses

   When they are used to mean a large number, they do have a plural form, which can be used as a partitive.

   *There are **millions** of pebbles on the beach.*
   *I saw **dozens** of children in the playground.*

Foreign plurals

Nouns that have come into English from foreign languages can:

- keep the plural form of the language they come from.

an axis	*two axes*
a crisis	*two crises*

- have plurals formed according to the rules for plural in English.

a thesaurus	*several thesauruses*
	(instead of thesauri)

- have two plurals: one from the foreign language and the other formed according to the rules for plural formation in English. The foreign plural is usually kept for scientific or specialized use.

an index	*some indexes/indices*
a formula	*some formulas/formulae*

Verbal nouns

The **verbal noun** is the -*ing* form, i.e. the present participle of the verb, used as a noun. It can be used in all the places that a noun can be used, but still keeps some characteristics of the verb. It is sometimes called the **gerund**.

> The **screaming** of the brakes terrified me.
> **Smoking** is prohibited.

The verbal noun normally functions as an uncountable noun, as above. However, there are some uses of the verbal noun that can be preceded by an indefinite article or used in the plural.

> He gave **a reading** from his latest volume of poetry.
> The **takings** were down this week in the shop.

The verbal noun can be preceded by the definite article, by adjectives, and by possessives.

> Her marvellous **singing** won Helen the scholarship.

Just like any noun, the verbal noun can function:

– as a **subject**.

> **Driving** was impossible.

– as the **complement** of the verb *be*.

> Seeing is **believing**.
> His greatest pleasure is **working**.

– as an **object** after certain verbs. See also p. 130.

> Louisa likes **swimming** but Helen prefers **diving**.

– after **prepositions** to make a prepositional phrase.

> *Can you watch them **without laughing**?*

Verbal nouns are also used:

– after some phrasal verbs such as: *be for/against, give up, keep on, look forward to, put off*.

> *She was all for **leaving** immediately.*
> *Linda gave up **swimming** but she kept on **dieting**.*
> *They were looking forward to **writing** home.*

– after certain set expressions such as: *can't stand, can't help, it's no use/good*.

> *I can't stand **waiting** around.*
> *I can't help **getting** cross.*
> *It's no use **crying** over spilt milk.*

The **possessive determiner** can be used with the verbal noun, especially in formal English.

> *Anna left the house without **my knowing**.*

• The verbal noun also has:

– a perfect form: ***having ...ed***.

> *Martin was accused of **having cheated**.*

– a passive form: ***being ...ed***.

> ***Being asked** did not bother me.*

– a perfect passive form: ***having been ...ed***.

> *The car showed no sign of **having been touched**.*

Determiners

Determiners are words that make the reference of nouns more specific. If I say '*this* car' it is clear that I mean a particular car which is near me. If I change it to '*my* car' I am saying something quite specific about ownership.

Determiners can be divided into several kinds according to:

– their meaning.

– what they may go with and where they may come in the noun phrase.

There are eight classes of determiner:

– the indefinite article *a* or *an*. See p. 162.

> *A* man came into the shop.
> *An* honest person would return the car to the owner.

– the definite article *the*. See p. 164.

> *The* dog chased *the* rabbit.

– the demonstratives *this*, *that*, *these*, *those*. See p. 168.

> *This* book is better than *that* one.
> *These* apples are redder than *those* ones.

– the possessives *my*, *your*, *his*, *her*, *its*, *our*, *their*. See p. 209.

> I gave *my* share to *her* sister.
> Shona found *his* book in *her* car.

– the quantifiers *some*, *any*, *enough*, *no*, *all*, *both*, *half*, *double*, *several*, *much*, *many*, *more*, *most*, *few*, *fewer*, *fewest*, *a few*, *little* (meaning not much), *less*, *least*, *a little*. See pp. 171–177.

> I've got **some** coffee but I haven't got **any** sugar.
> Have you got **much** money on you?
> There were **no** witnesses to the accident.
> **Both** girls saw the attack.
> **Few** people know the answer to that.
> The safety net gives **little** help to those who need it most.

– the numbers, cardinal (*one*, *two*, *three*...), and ordinal (*first*, *second*, *third*...). See p. 176.

> There's **one** thing I need to ask you.
> The **two** boys grew up together in Manhattan.
> **Three** men were found hiding in the building.
> Their **second** child is due in October.
> She lost in the **third** round of the tournament.

– the distributives *each*, *every*, *either*, *neither*. See p. 178.

> **Each** child received a book.
> **Every** girl was given a number to wear.
> **Either** book should help you with the problem.

– the exclamatives *what*, *such*. See p. 180.

> **What** nonsense!
> **What** a shame!
> They make **such** a fuss over small things!

Generally, a noun phrase has only one determiner in it, or none at all. See p. 160. A few determiners, e.g. *all*, *both*, and the numbers, can be used together with another determiner. See p. 160.

The indefinite article

The indefinite article is *a* or *an*. The form *an* is used before a word that starts with a vowel sound.

> *a* girl   *a* cat
> *an* eight-year-old girl   *an* engineer

The indefinite article is used with singular countable nouns:

– to refer to a person or a thing that you are mentioning for the first time in a conversation or a piece of writing.

> *A* man was seen driving away in *a* black car.

– to refer to a person or a thing which you do not want to be specific about.

> I stopped off at *a* shop to buy *a* newspaper.
> You go past *a* petrol station on the left, and then you'll see our house on the right.

– to refer to a person or a thing which you cannot be more specific about because there is not enough information.

> *A* man called to see you this afternoon.
> There was *a* telephone call for you a minute ago.

– in definitions.

> *An* octopus is *a* sea creature with eight tentacles.

– when you refer to a person's profession.

> Her father is *a* dentist and her mother is *a* teacher.

– to express a quantity, unless you wish to emphasize the number, when *one* must be used. The equivalent for plural nouns is *some* or no determiner at all. See p. 160.

> I want *a* needle and *a* thimble.
> Would you like *a* glass of wine?
> There is only **one** glass of wine left in the bottle.
> Guy has bought *a* skateboard.
> We've got three pairs of rollerblades and **one** skateboard.

It is the sound, not the spelling, that decides where *an* is used. For example, although *unique* begins with a vowel, the sound at the beginning resembles a *y*- sound.

> *an* idiot   *an* awful mistake
> *a* unicorn   *a* unique experience

> There are a few words that begin with a silent *h-*, in front of which **an** should be used. They are: *heir, heiress, honest, honour, hour.*

• Very formal or old-fashioned speakers also use the *an* form with some words beginning with an *h-* that is not silent, especially *historical* and *hotel*.

> I waited **an** hour.
> They joined *a* historical society.
> They joined **an** historical society. (old-fashioned English)
> They were staying at *a* hotel.
> They were staying at **an** hotel. (old-fashioned English)

The definite article

The definite article is **the**.

The definite article is used with singular and plural nouns. It is used both with countable nouns and uncountable nouns:

- to make definite or specific reference to a person or a thing that has already been referred to.

    *There's **the** man I was telling you about!*

- to refer to a person or thing that is already specific because of what those talking already know. In the first example below, '*the children*' would be members of our family and '*the swimming pool*' is the swimming pool we normally go to.

    *Let's take **the** children to **the** swimming pool.*
    *Did you switch **the** heating on?*
    *There were drinks in **the** fridge but **the** beer was soon finished.*

- to generalize about a whole class or species, usually of plants or animals. A singular noun is used for this purpose. The first example means '*The elephant species is hunted.*'

    ***The** elephant is still hunted for its tusks.*
    ***The** snowdrop **is** the first flower to arrive in the new year.*

- when it is followed by an adjective used as a noun indicating nationality or when generalizing about a whole class of people. *The Dutch* in the first example means '*Dutch people in general*'.

    ***The Dutch** are very skilful engineers.*
    ***The poor** were crowding the streets of the capital.*
    ***The homeless** were sheltered in the church.*

– before the names of rivers, groups of islands, seas, oceans, and mountain ranges.

> **The** *Thames* **The** *Hebrides*
> **The** *North Sea* **The** *Pacific*

– before the names of certain public institutions, most newspapers, and some magazines.

> **The** *British Museum* **The** *Hilton Hotel*
> **The** *Lyceum Theatre* **The** *Houses of Parliament*
> **The** *Independent* **The** *Guardian*
> **The** *Listener* **The** *New Scientist*

– before parts of the body when these are referred to in an impersonal way.

> *A stone struck him on **the hand**.*
> *Martin hit him on **the head**.*

• The definite article is rarely used with titles. Proper nouns that refer to persons, such as *Sue* and *Ron*, and proper nouns used in conjunction with titles, such as *Queen Elizabeth*, *Doctor Thomas*, and *Captain Parry*, only take a definite article if:

– they stand for the name of a thing such as a boat.

> **The Queen Elizabeth II** *is on a long cruise.*

– a distinction is being made between people who have identical names. This use can give emphasis to the noun.

> *Ah, no.* **The David Parry I know** *lives in Manchester.*
> *I saw Paul Kay in town this morning. – Not* **the** *Paul Kay?*

Nouns used without a determiner

Certain noun phrases do not have a determiner at all.

We usually leave out the determiner when we use a noun or a noun phrase in the plural to make a generalization.

> He sells **cars** for a living.
> **Tigers** are nearing extinction.
> **Onions** are good for you.
> **Grassy hills** rise on all sides of the town.

Singular nouns that are uncountable are used without a determiner when you are making a general reference.

> New **information** is now available.
> Do you like **jelly**?
> This shop sells **furniture**.

- This is particularly true when the uncountable noun is used for the first time in a general way in the course of a conversation or piece of writing. They can be used with a determiner when the reference becomes specific. For example, you can ask someone if they like *cake* as a rule, and then ask the person if she would like some of *your cake*.

> **The** information she gave me was inaccurate.
> Would you like some of **the jelly** I made for the party?
> We don't let the dog climb onto **the** furniture.

There are a number of idiomatic expressions that usually omit a determiner. Examples are expressions that refer to:

- travel, when you proceed **by**: *bicycle, car, bus, train, ship, boat, plane.*

> Anna went **by bicycle** but Lucy went **by car**.
> He was chased by police **on foot**.

– time with the prepositions *at*, **before**, or **by**, *dawn, sunrise, sunset, noon, midnight, night, supper, dinner, day, night*.

> *Catherine rose **at dawn** and went to bed **at sunset**.*
> *We swam in the pool **by day** and partied **by night**.*

– meals: to have *breakfast, tea, lunch*.

> *Jane had **breakfast** at home.*
> *She met Diana **for lunch**.*

– institutions, with the prepositions **to** or **at**: *church, hospital, prison, school, work*.

> *John was taken **to hospital** with a broken ankle.*
> *Lucy has been kept late **at school** today.*
> *Ruth was **at home** all day.*

– seasons of the year, when you are generalizing, e.g: *in spring, in summer, in autumn, in winter*.

> ***In autumn**, the grapes are harvested by hand.*
> *The place is packed **in summer**.*

However, all of these words are used with the definite article when you are talking about a specific time, place, season, etc.

> *Philip travelled by **the same train** as Mehandra.*
> *Just look at **the wonderful sunset**.*
> *Pam works at **the hospital**.*
> *I can't work well **in the summer**.*

Demonstratives

Demonstratives are used to specify the distance of something in space or time in relation to the speaker.

The **demonstratives** are: **this**, **that**, **these**, **those**.

This and **these** refer to objects near the speaker.

> **This apple** looks ripe.
> **These apples** come from Australia.

The reference may be nearness in time, especially future time.

> I'll call round **this** afternoon.
> The festival ends **this** Thursday.
> **This** summer is the warmest I can remember.

That and **those** refer to objects that are further away from the speaker.

> I think **that boy** over there is lost.
> Can you see **those people** up on the hill?

This and **that** are used before singular countable nouns and uncountable nouns.

> I can touch **this picture**, but I can't reach **that one**.
> **This book** is mine, but **that magazine** isn't.

These and **those** are used before plural countable nouns.

> I'm peeling **these potatoes** for a shepherd's pie.
> **Those men** are mending the roof.

Possessives

Possessives are used to specify the ownership of an item, or, if the noun refers to something animate, to specify a relationship.

> That is **my car**.
> Mr Smith was **my teacher** in the sixth form.

The form of the possessive changes according to the number and gender of the person or thing that possesses the item.

> **His brothers** all came to the wedding.
> **Their aunt** lives in London, but **their cousins** live in Berlin.
> **Your shoes** are under **your bed**.

person	singular	plural
1st	**my**	**our**
2nd	**your**	**your**
3rd (masculine)	**his**	**their**
3rd (feminine)	**her**	**their**
3rd (neuter)	**its**	**their**

Possessive determiners, which can go into a noun phrase, are not the same as possessive pronouns (*mine, hers, yours,* etc.), which can stand alone. See p. 144.

Another sort of possessive is the **possessive phrase**.

This acts just like a possessive word but is a noun or noun phrase ending in **-'s** or **-s'**. A possessive phrase acts as a possessive determiner, but may itself include one of the other determiners.

Robert's mother

the **visitors'** washroom

a good **day's** work

the **Prime Minister's** press secretary

Sally's new job

the **residents'** dining room

my wife's cousin

Quantifiers

Quantifiers are used to indicate the amount or quantity of something referred to by a noun. They are different from numbers because they indicate an approximate amount rather than an exact amount. They can be grouped according to their use.

all, some, any, much, enough, no

- You can use **all**, **some**, **any**, or **enough**, before a plural countable noun or an uncountable noun.

  *Can I have **some** chips, please?*
  *Anna gave me **all** her money.*
  *Peter never has **any** time to visit us.*

  You can use **no** before a singular or a plural countable noun or an uncountable noun.

  *There were **no** pictures of the party.*
  *There is **no** hospital in this town.*
  ***No** information has been released yet.*

- **Some**, **any**, **much**, and **enough** are used to refer to a part of the item.

  *Would you like **some** ice cream?*
  *We didn't have **much** success.*
  *I haven't seen **enough** evidence to convince me.*
  *I couldn't find **any** fresh milk at the shop.*

  All and **no** refer to the whole of the item.

  ***All the milk** has been used.*
  *There is **no milk** in the fridge.*

– **Some** is used in positive sentences.

> I've bought **some** chocolate.
> I saw **some** lovely shoes in town this morning.

– **Any** is used in negative sentences.

> I didn't buy **any** chocolate this week.
> I haven't seen **any** birds in the garden today.

• In questions, **any** is used when there is no particular expectation about the answer; **some** is used when the answer is expected to be positive.

> Have you got **any** fresh bread?
> Has Paul heard **any** news about the accident?
> Would you like **some** cake, Aisha?

• The use of **no** with *there is/are* is very common.

> **There was no post** today.
> There are **no jobs** available for electricians at the moment.

half, double, both

– **Half** can be used with countable nouns and with uncountable nouns.

> **Half the time** I didn't understand what was going on.
> **Half the students** came from overseas.

– **Double** is used with uncountable nouns.

> We're going to need **double the present supply** of water.
> They want **double the money** they originally asked for.

– **Both** is used to define two things represented by a plural countable noun.

> **Both men** were given another chance.
> **Both dogs** had to be put down.

See p. 161 for more information about quantifiers when they are used with other determiners.

The following quantifiers are used to express **graded** amounts of an item (e.g. whether there is more or less of something).

> Have you seen **many tourists** in town?
> Yes, I've seen **more tourists** than usual.
> I think **most tourists** just stay for a couple of days.

> I didn't put **much petrol** in the car.
> I think we need **more petrol**.
> The news caused **much excitement**.
> **Most information** about our services is available on the Internet.

– **Many**, **more**, **most** are used with graded quantities of plural countable nouns.

> Have you seen **many tourists** in town?
> Yes, I've seen **more tourists** than usual.
> I think **most tourists** just stay for a couple of days.

– **Much**, **more**, **most** are used with graded quantities of uncountable nouns.

> I didn't put **much petrol** in the car.
> I think we need **more petrol**.
> The news caused **much excitement**.
> **Most information** about our services is available on the Internet.

- *Few*, *fewer*, *fewest* are used with graded quantities of plural countable nouns.

> *Few people* know the answer to this problem.
> *Fewer loans* are being granted than usual.
> Japanese workers take *the fewest holidays*.

- *Little*, *less*, *least* are used with graded quantities of uncountable nouns.

> There is *little chance* of rain today.
> This technique causes *less harm* to the environment.
> I need to get from one place to another with *the least inconvenience*.

• *A few*, and *a little* are different from *few* and *little* on their own because they have a positive sense. *Few* means 'not many',

> *Few* buildings survived the earthquake.

but *a few* means 'several'.

> *A few kind people* helped the injured man.
> *A few delays* are inevitable.

Little means 'not much',

> The students were given very *little help* with their projects.
> Edward got *little encouragement* from his parents.

but *a little* means 'some'.

> I need *a little help* from my friends.
> Everyone needs *a little encouragement* now and then.
> Do you take sugar? – Just *a little*, please.

Few and little are often used in a negative sense to suggest disappointment or pessimism, while a few and a little are used in a positive sense to suggest that things are better than they might have been.

Numbers

There are two common kinds of number:

Cardinal numbers are used in all forms of counting that involve a total.

> **one** chair   **two** chairs
> **a hundred** people   **ten thousand** pounds

Ordinal numbers are used to talk about where something is placed in an ordered sequence. They are often used right after the definite article or after a possessive.

> **The first** horse in was disqualified.
> He's celebrating **his fifty-first** birthday in August.
> The company has just celebrated **its one hundred and fiftieth**
>   anniversary.

Ordinals are mostly formed by adding **-th** to a cardinal number.

> fourth   twentieth   hundredth
> fifth   forty-ninth   millionth
> sixth   eighty-sixth   thousandth
> nine hundred and ninety ninth

Some examples of exceptions are the words *first*, *second*, and *third*, and combinations which contain them, such as *twenty-first*.

Cardinal numbers can be used at the beginning of a noun phrase, like determiners.

> **one** chair   **two** chairs
> **a hundred** people   **ten thousand** pounds

or on their own, like pronouns.

> *And then there were* **three**.
> **Four** *of them came towards us.*
> *The other* **two** *went to get help.*

- Grammatically speaking, the words *next*, *last*, and *another* can also be regarded as ordinal numbers.

> *It rained on the* **last** *day of our holiday.*
> *The* **next** *horse in was declared the winner.*
> *Oh no, not* **another** *birthday!*

Ordinal numbers and the words *next* and *last* are sometimes called **postdeterminers**, since they come after the word **the** or a possessive .

> *The* **next** *three days are going to be very exciting.*
> *The* **last** *three years have been difficult for everyone.*
> *We have to get off the bus at the* **next** *stop.*

- An ordinal, as well as *next*, *last*, and *another*, can be used together with a cardinal number in the same noun phrase.

> *The* **first three** *correct entries will win a prize.*
> *He scored* **another three** *goals before the end of the match.*

- To show that a cardinal number is only approximate, the word, *some* is often used before it.

> **Some two hundred** *people gathered in the pouring rain.*

Distributives

Distributives are determiners that are used to talk about how something is shared out or divided.

The distributives are *each*, *every*, *either*, and *neither*. They are used with a singular noun.

> *Each child* was given a balloon.
> I remember *every detail* of our conversation.
> *Either child* could win the prize.
> *Neither plan* was successful.

– *Each* and *every* are not used with proper nouns.

– *Each* is used to refer to separate persons or things in a group of two or more.

> Four girls came and *each one* sang a song.
> *Each ticket* should have a number on the back.

– *Every* is used to refer to all the persons or things in a group of three or more.

> *Every teacher* has a key to the building.
> Katrina danced with *every boy* at the party.

– *Every* can be used in front of ordinal numbers. 'Every second house' means *the second house, the fourth house, the sixth house,* and so on.

> I have to work *every third weekend*.
> *Every fourth house* has a garage.

- **Either** is used to talk about one of two people or things.

    *They did not appoint **either** man as captain.*
    ***Either** restaurant would suit me.*

- **Neither** is used to exclude both of two people or things that are being referred to.

    *They appointed **neither** man as captain.*
    ***Neither** restaurant is cheap enough.*

Exclamatives

Exclamatives are used to introduce an exclamation of surprise, admiration, or a similar emotion.

The exclamatives are: **what**, **such**.

Exclamations introduced by one of these words consist either of:

- the exclamative in a noun phrase alone (usually with *What...*).

    What *a laugh!*
    What *awful weather!*

- the exclamative and its noun phrase in a complete clause.

    He is **such** *a nice man!*
    You always wear **such** *lovely things!*
    What *a pleasant surprise this is!*

Noun phrases with several determiners

Most noun phrases contain only one determiner or none at all, but if there are more, they follow a definite order. Determiners can be divided into four groups, depending on what other determiners they can be used with and the order that they follow.

There are two large groups:

A *the, this, these, that, those, a(n)*, and the possessives *my, your, her, his,* etc.

> **a** *ripe orange*　　　　**my** *young sister*
> **this** *ripe orange*　　　**our** *young sister*

B *another, some, any, no, either, neither, each, enough, a few, a little.*

> **each** *ripe orange*　　　**another** *sister*
> **some** *ripe oranges*　　　**enough** *money*

The words in groups A and B are known as the **central determiners**. A noun phrase will normally contain only one central determiner.

- The group A and group B words cannot be used together, with the exception that words in group B may be followed by a group A word if *of* is placed between them.

> **some of those** *oranges*　　　**neither of my** *sisters*

- Words in group A can be used in combination with determiners in groups C and D (below).

> **Both** *girls were reading.*
> **Both my** *young sisters are really naughty.*
> **All** *visitors must now leave the ship.*
> **All the** *visitors left the ship.*

There are two smaller groups.

C The smallest group consists of the words: *all, both, half, double,* and *twice.* These can be used on their own before a noun or before the group A determiners above. Some speakers of English prefer to insert *of* between *all, both,* or *half* and a central determiner.

> **All of the** visitors left the ship.
> **Half of the** oranges will have to be thrown away.

- The words in group C are sometimes called **predeterminers**. The exclamatives *such* and *what* belong to this group. See p. 180 for more details about these.

D The words in the fourth group are, *every, many, several, few, little, much, more, most, less,* the ordinal numbers *first, second, third* etc., and *last.* These can be used on their own before a noun,

> **Every** move was carefully recorded.
> She did **many** kind things.
> She has **few** friends.
> **Last** orders, please.

or after the A group of determiners.

> **Your every** move is being watched.
> **The many** kind things she did went unnoticed.
> **Her few** possessions had been stolen.
> **The first** thing she did was call her mother.
> I would rather forget **these last** few days.

Adjectives

Adjectives are used with nouns to make the meaning more specific.
If you use the noun *'bear'* it can mean any animal of that species.
As soon as you say *'a large, brown bear'* you have given two of its
attributes (colour and size). A noun is said to be **modified** by its
adjectives.

Adjectives have two main features:

– Most adjectives can go before a noun; this is known as their
   attributive use.

> a **tall** girl
> **green** grass
> four **badly behaved little** boys

– Most adjectives can also go after a link verb such as *be* or *seem*; this is
   known as their **predicative** use.

> The roses are **yellow**.
> The girls are getting **tall**.
> These books seem really **interesting**.

Any word that can go into both of these positions is a normal adjective.
When used predicatively (after a link verb), an adjective can either
describe the **subject** of a sentence,

> The roses are **yellow**.
> The girls are getting **tall**.
> These books are really **interesting**.

or the **object** of the sentence. See also p. 11.

> Anna painted the room **green**.
> The children drove him **mad**.

Adjective order

The order is normally:

– adjectives that describe feelings or qualities.

> **pleasant** childhood memories
> **beautiful** brown hands

– adjectives of size, age, temperature, or measurement.

> some **hot** scones
> a **rectangular** pie dish
> those **nice young** girls
> a **lovely big** smile

– adjectives of colour.

> the **green** hills of home
> smart **brown** shoes
> her beautiful **blue** eyes

– adjectives of nationality or origin.

> those friendly **Spanish** girls
> both the small grey **Irish** horses
> an elegant **French** woman

– adjectives denoting the substance or material that something is made from.

> a large **wooden** door
> an elegant **silver** teapot

It is possible to pile up adjectives in English, but in practice more than four is uncommon.

> *a **happy young blonde German** girl*
> ***beautiful old English half-timbered** houses*

- Adjectives before a noun are not usually separated by *and*, unless they are adjectives of colour.

> *a **green and white** striped shirt*
> *a **red and blue** flag*

- Adjectives can themselves be premodified by adverbs of degree. See also p. 186.

> *an **extremely intelligent** student*
> *a **very tall** man*
> *a **fairly untidy** flat*

Some adjectives can only be used predicatively (i.e. after a link verb such as *be*). Many of the members of this group begin with *a-*:

> *afloat, afraid, alike, alive, alone, ashamed, asleep, awake.*

> *Our balloon was **aloft** at last.*
> *Charles is **abroad** again.*
> *The child is **afraid**.*
> *The girls were **asleep** and were not **aware** of the noise.*

When an adjective is used predicatively it may have to be followed by a particular preposition if the phrase continues.

> *She was glad.*   *She was **glad to** help.*
> *He was afraid.*   *He was **afraid for** his life.*
> *I was free.*   *I was **free from** guilt.*
> *It is **devoid of** interest.*   *He was **intent on** revenge.*

There are some adjectives such as *devoid (of)*, *intent (on)* that always have to have a following phrase.

Although attributive adjectives usually come before the noun that they modify, there are some that can go immediately after the noun, particularly when they are used with plural nouns, e.g. *absent*, *present*, *involved*, *concerned*. When these adjectives are used in this position they may have a different meaning from the one that they have when they come before the noun.

> ***Everyone present*** *was given tea.*
> *The* ***present government*** *took over four years ago.*
> *The* ***people absent*** *from work were all ill.*
> *Let us toast* ***absent friends****.*
> *The* ***dealers concerned*** *were sent to jail.*
> *There were letters from* ***concerned parents****.*

* There are some set phrases which always have an adjective immediately after the noun.

> the ***Princess Royal***   *a* ***lion rampant***
> the ***president elect***   *the* ***Attorney General***

Premodifiers and postmodifiers

Adjectives, determiners, and other nouns can all be used to describe a noun more specifically; that is, they can be used as **modifiers**. Nouns can also be modified by prepositional groups (groups of words that begin with a preposition) and relative clauses added after the noun. See p. 270 for more about relative clauses.

To make it simpler to talk about any modifying word which comes in front of a noun, we can use the term **premodifier**.

a young man	**these** onions
my aunt's house	**the elephant** house

Those modifiers that come after the noun are called **postmodifiers**.

the young man **with the guitar**
the person **who met me**
the girl **I was standing near**
the people **involved**

Comparison

The **comparative** form of an adjective is commonly used to compare two people, things, or states, when you want to say that one thing has a larger or smaller amount of a quality than another.

- If the second part of the comparison is mentioned it follows **than**.

    *Anna is **taller than** Mary but Mary is **older**.*
    *Emma is much **slimmer than** when I last saw her.*
    *Online learning is **less expensive than** conventional college
        courses.*

- Comparison in which you are considering whether two people or things are equal is shown by using **as...as** in the affirmative and **not as...as** or **not so...as** in the negative.

    *Helen is **as tall as** Linda, but **not as strong**.*

The **superlative** form is used for more than two people, things, or states, when one thing has qualities that exceed all the others. Superlative adjectives have **the** in front of them, but it can be omitted in predicative positions.

    *That is **the smallest** camera I have ever seen.*
    *He gave **the least expensive** gift to his sister.*
    *I'll have whichever is (the) **ripest**.*

There are two ways in which the comparative and superlative forms of adjectives are formed:

- You add **-er** (comparative) or **-est** (superlative) to the adjective. Adjectives with one syllable usually take these endings.

	comparative	superlative
bright	**brighter**	the **brightest**
long	**longer**	the **longest**
sharp	**sharper**	the **sharpest**

- If the word already ends in **-e**, the **-e** must be left off. If a word ends in **-y**, it usually takes **-er** or **-est**, and the **-y** changes to **-i**.

	comparative	superlative
wise	**wiser**	the **wisest**
pretty	**prettier**	the **prettiest**
weary	**wearier**	the **weariest**

- You add the word **more** or **most** in front of the adjective. Adjectives with three syllables or more use **more** or **most** in front of the adjective.

	comparative	superlative
fortunate	**more** fortunate	the **most** fortunate
relevant	**more** relevant	the **most** relevant

Adjectives formed from participles use **more** or **most** as well.

	comparative	superlative
provoking	**more** provoking	the **most** provoking
enthralled	**more** enthralled	the **most** enthralled

To indicate the opposite of both the **-er/-est** and the **more/most** forms of comparison, **less** or **least** is always used.

	comparative	superlative
sharp	**less** sharp	the **least** sharp
fortunate	**less** fortunate	the **least** fortunate
interesting	**less** interesting	the **least** interesting
involved	**less** involved	the **least** involved

Adjectives with two syllables (including those that already end in **-er**) can follow either pattern or sometimes both patterns. If you are doubtful about a two-syllable adjective, use the **more/most** pattern.

	comparative	superlative
shallow	**shallower**	the **shallowest**
or	**more** shallow	the **most** shallow
polite	**politer**	the **politest**
or	**more** polite	the **most** polite

A small group of irregular adjectives have quite different forms for the comparative and superlative forms.

	comparative	superlative
good	**better**	the **best**
bad	**worse**	the **worst**
far	**further**	the **furthest**

Adverbs and adverbials

When you want to add information about *how*, *when*, *where*, or *to what extent* something has happened, you can use an **adverbial**. Many adverbials are members of the group of words called **adverbs**, but adverbials are not necessarily just single words. They can also be word groups, prepositional phrases, or even clauses. They are sometimes called **adjuncts**.

Adverbials generally modify the meaning of a verb,

> I **greatly** admire your courage.
> They changed **hurriedly into their pyjamas**.
> Monica hummed **softly as she washed the car**.
> The firework exploded **with a loud bang**.
> He ran **across the lawn towards the house**.

an adjective,

> Harry is **absolutely** terrified of flying.
> You must admit that he can be **rather** boring.
> That is **quite** silly.
> Fears like that are **very** real to the sufferer.

another adverb,

> I thought about it **quite** seriously.
> The children are behaving **remarkably** well.
> Ali objected **very** strongly to the plan.

a whole sentence,

> **Frankly**, I think he is lying.
> **Nevertheless**, we must give him a chance.
> **Honestly**, I didn't mean to be rude to you.

or a prepositional phrase.

> *We are **really in a no-win situation**.*

Most adverbials are optional parts of a clause or phrase, but there are a few verbs that need an adverb to complete their meaning. See p. 81. Conditional sentences must also have an adverbial clause, usually one beginnining with *if* or **unless**. See p. 267 for more about adverbial clauses.

Adverbials can be divided into:

- adverbials of **manner**, which express *how*: e.g. *slowly, with care, well*.

  > *Two men were working their way **slowly** up the hillside.*

- adverbials of **place**, which express *where*: e.g. *there, here, up, in town*.

  > *Two men were working their way **up the hillside**.*

- adverbials of **time**, which express *when*: e.g. *now, today, last night, lately*.

  > *Two men were lost on the hills **yesterday**.*

- adverbials of **degree**, which express *to what extent*: e.g. *largely, extremely, much, by a whisker*.

  > *It was **largely** their own fault.*

- adverbials of **frequency**, which express *how often*: e.g. *rarely, often, sometimes, twice daily*.

  > *Search parties went out **every hour**.*

Although adverbials change the meaning of clauses or phrases, they are usually optional parts of the group or clause.

> He coughed **nervously**.
> **Really**, I think you are mistaken.
> **In a fit of temper**, he slammed the door shut.

They stand outside the word, group, or clause that they are associated with. For example, the same adverb can in one sentence be part of the description of a verb, while in another sentence, it may modify the whole clause.

> I think she acted **honestly**.
> **Honestly**, who does she think she is?

The exceptions are that:

– Some verbs must be followed by an adverbial to complete their meaning.

> Alice behaved **wonderfully**.
> Sylvia acted **unlawfully**.
> Justin sped **down the corridor**.

– Some verbs require both an object and an adverbial to complete their meaning. See also p. 28.

> Ranjit put the folder **back**.
> James stood the golf clubs **in the corner**.
> Clare placed the cover **over the cot**.

• New meanings can be made by combining an adverbial with a verb to make a phrasal verb. See also p. 81 for more about phrasal verbs.

> The car **pulled out**.
> Lydia **went away**.
> Things **are looking up**.

Adverbials are classified according to the way they modify a word, group or clause. In addition to the uses given on p. 191, one important use of a special group of adverbials is to show how a sentence relates to what comes before it. An adverb used in this way is called a **sentence adverb**.

> **Nevertheless**, we must give him an answer.
> **However**, it's good advice.
> **On the other hand**, we cannot turn him down.

Another use of adverbials is to let your listener or reader know your point of view about a situation. This is called a **viewpoint adverb**.

> **Foolishly**, I gave him my address.
> **Clearly**, he deserves our help.
> **Actually**, I don't mind.

A further group of adverbials, all of them adverbs of degree, can only be used with adjectives or other adverbs. Examples are *very, rather, quite, really, too, somewhat*. These are sometimes called **submodifiers** because they can weaken or strengthen the descriptive value of the adjective.

> She seems **rather** nice.
> Angus is a **very** good tennis player.
> Kim gave me this **really** expensive bag.

They are used mainly with adjectives of quality. An adverb can also be submodified by another adverb.

> She began to cry, **quite loudly**.
> Sometimes I think you're **too easily** impressed.
> It must have been done **extremely recently**.
> The car was **almost totally** submerged in the flood water.

There are certain adverbs (and adverbials) which can only be used with verbs and so cannot modify adjectives.

- Most adverbs are able to come:

- before the verb phrase or the subject

> **Happily** she ran over the sand dunes.
> **Tearfully**, he told his brother the whole story.

- after the verb phrase or the object

> She ran **happily** over the sand dunes.
> He was telling the whole story **tearfully** to his brother.

- between the auxiliary and the main verb.

> She was **happily** running about over the sand dunes.
> He was **tearfully** telling the whole story to his brother.

- Some adverbs can only come **after** the verb, e.g. back, up, down, sideways, clockwise.

> Suddenly the frightened animal ran **back**.
> They hammered the wedge in **sideways**.

- A few adverbs can come **before** the main verb, e.g. barely, hardly, little, rarely, scarcely, seldom.

> **Scarcely had she spoken** when it came crashing down.
> He **had hardly eaten** anything.
> **Seldom** have I seen such ridiculous behaviour.

A subordinate clause that begins with one of these words adopts the same word order as a question. These are called **broad negatives**, because they give a negative meaning to a clause.

Compare:

*They **never noticed** her presence.*
*They **scarcely noticed** her presence.*

Some speakers take care not to place an adverb between the *to* and the **base form** of the verb in a *'to* **infinitive**'. This is called a 'split infinitive'. There is no good reason to regard a split infinitive as an error; the choice is a matter of personal preference.

> *I need to **really** think hard about this.*
> *I **really** need to think hard about this.*

Adverbs with nouns and pronouns

While **adverbs** can modify most parts of speech, they normally do not modify **nouns** or **pronouns**. Much more common is the use of an adverb of degree to modify a whole **noun phrase**.

> *Dominic thought that Geoffrey was **rather a good teacher**.*
> *Jason is **quite a skilled craftsman**.*

There is a small group of adverbs that can modify nouns and indefinite pronouns.

> *the **man downstairs***
> *the **example above***
> ***Almost everyone** brought a bottle to the party.*

Form of adverbs

Most **adverbs** are formed by adding **-ly** to the end of the related adjective.

slow	slowly
clever	cleverly
annual	annually

Exceptionally, words which end in **-ble** drop off the **-e** before **-ly** is added. So do the words *true* and *due*.

sensible	sensibly
suitable	suitably
true	truly
due	duly

A common spelling mistake is to add **-ley**. This mistake is often made when the adjective ends in the letter **-e**. Note the correct spelling of adverbs formed from adjectives ending in **-e**.

extreme	extremely
divine	divinely
free	freely

Adjectives that end in **-y** change to **-i** before adding **-ly**, unless, like *sly* or *dry*, they have only one syllable.

happy	happily
greedy	greedily
sly	slyly

Some adverbs keep the same spelling as the adjective to which they are related. It is often difficult to tell at first whether the word is an adjective or an adverb. The general rule is to look at the other words which it occurs with. If it comes before a noun it is probably an adjective.

> *a **short way***   *a **late meeting***
> *a **long pause***   *an **early lecture***

If it relates to a verb or an adjective it is probably an adverb.

> *The lesson **was cut short**.*
> *We **met late** at night.*
> *Don't **stay long**.*
> *He **came in early**.*

Some adverbs have the same spelling as a preposition. They can be told apart if you look at the words they are found with. Prepositions are normally used in front of noun phrases, because prepositions must have an object.

> *He rushed **in an attempt** to catch his bus.*
> *She hurried **over her meal** because she was late.*

When the word is found without an object, especially at the end of a clause, it will usually be an adverb.

> *He rushed **in**.*
> *She hurried **over**.*

Just like certain adjectives, some adverbs have comparative and superlative forms and can be used with submodifiers.

*Kim treated Sharon **well**, Karen **less well** and Janice*
*   **the least well**.*
*Malcolm walked **the most slowly** of all of them.*
*Tariq acted **very kindly** towards him.*
*You must behave **far more sensibly** in future.*
*This graph shows that girls performed **the best** at maths*
*   this year.*

Superlative forms of adverbs are quite rare.

Pronouns

A **pronoun** is a word that is used in the place of a noun or a whole noun phrase.

Pronouns are commonly used:

– in place of a noun or a noun phrase that has already been mentioned, when the repetition of the noun or noun phrase would be very strange.

> *Sam has to go to the airport. Can you give **him** a lift?*
> *The young prince and his wife came out on to the balcony.*
>   ***They** waved to the crowd.*
> *The mechanic tested the starter motor. **It** would not work.*
>   ***He** tried **it** again.*

– when we know perfectly well who or what is referred to. When, for example, I use the pronoun *I* it is because it would be unusual to refer to myself by name.

> *I'm sorry **I**'m late.*
> ***We**'d better ring and say **we**'re not coming.*

– when the name of someone or something is not known.

> ***He**'s the man who came to the house yesterday!*
> ***Who**'s she?*

Types of pronoun

There are seven different types of pronoun, classified according to their meaning and use.

The **personal** pronouns can be used as subject or object in a clause.

> *He gave her a box of chocolates.*
> *We saw them both on Friday.*
> *I can see you!*

The **reflexive** pronouns are used in object position when the action of a verb is performed on the subject by the subject. They are obligatory with certain verbs.

> *The puppy entangled itself in the lead.*
> *I've just cut myself on a piece of glass.*

Reflexive pronouns are also used for emphasis.

> *Never mind. I'll do it myself.*
> *The professor himself did not know the answer.*

The **possessive** pronouns indicate ownership.

> *Give it back, it's mine.*
> *Perhaps it really is theirs after all.*

The **demonstrative** pronouns indicate items that are near to or far from us.

> *This is Betty's and that is Peter's.*
> *These are nice. Where did you find them?*

The **relative** pronouns are used to link a modifying clause to a noun phrase or to a clause.

> *I don't know what you mean.*
> *That's the girl who always comes top.*

The **interrogative** pronouns are used to ask a question about the noun phrase they stand in for.

> **What** would you like for lunch?
> **Which** is the fresh milk?
> **Who** was responsible?

The **indefinite** pronouns are used for a broad range of reference when it is not necessary or not possible to use a personal pronoun.

> **Everyone** had a compass and a whistle.
> **Neither** wanted to give in and apologize.
> **Much** needs to be done.

Personal pronouns

Personal pronouns are used as the subject, object, or complement in a clause. They are commonly found taking the place of a noun phrase when it is mentioned for a second time.

person	subject	singular object	subject	plural object
1st	*I*	*me*	*we*	*us*
2nd	*you*	*you*	*you*	*you*
3rd masculine	*he*	*him*	*they*	*them*
3rd feminine	*she*	*her*	*they*	*them*
3rd neutral	*it*	*it*	*they*	*them*

We use the 1st person pronoun *I* to take the role of the speaker. The 2nd person pronoun **you** is used to take the role of the listener. In the case of **you**, there is only one pronoun to cover the singular and the plural, so that it is sometimes necessary to use a form of words that will make clear who is being addressed.

> **You** should be ashamed.
> **All of you** should be ashamed.
> **You** must **all** stop writing now.

When more than one personal pronoun is used with a verb, the order is normally: 3rd or 2nd person before 1st person; 2nd person before 3rd person.

> **She and I** do not get on very well.
> **You and he** should buy the boat between you.

When two pronouns or a personal noun and a personal pronoun are the joint subject of a verb, the subject form of the pronouns must be used. Avoid the common mistake of saying, for example, *Jerry and me are...*

> **Jerry and I** *are going to paint the house ourselves.*
> **He** *and I are going to paint it.*
> **Melanie** *and I are going shopping.*

When either two pronouns or a noun plus a personal pronoun are the joint object of a verb, the object form of the pronoun must be used:

> *They decided to help* **Jane and me**.

The object form of a pronoun is used after a preposition. Avoid the common mistake of saying, for example, *between you and I*.

> *Between* **you** *and* **me**, *I don't like this place.*
> *Wasn't that kind of* **me**?

The object form is usual in everyday spoken usage. In formal and old-fashioned English, the subject form is used:

– after the verb *be*.

It's **me**.	Informal
It is **I**.	Formal/old-fashioned
I saw at once that it was **her**.	Informal
I saw at once that it was **she**.	Formal/old-fashioned

- after *than* in comparison with *be*.

> | *John is smaller **than him**.* | Informal |
> | *John is smaller **than he (is)**.* | Formal/old-fashioned |
> | *Sylvia is cleverer **than me**.* | Informal |
> | *Sylvia is cleverer **than I (am)**.* | Formal/old-fashioned |

Otherwise, *than* + **object** pronoun is necessary.

> *She's probably done more **than me**.*

• The object form is also used to supply short answers to questions.

> *Who found Gran's watch? – **Me**. Aren't I clever!*

Reflexive pronouns

Reflexive pronouns are used:

person	singular	plural
1st	myself	ourselves
2nd	yourself	yourselves
3rd masculine	himself	themselves
3rd feminine	herself	themselves
3rd neuter	itself	themselves
General	oneself	

– when the speaker or writer is referring to an action that he or she has caused to happen and of which he or she is also the object.

> *I cut **myself** with the carving knife.*
> *Sometimes I just don't like **myself** very much.*

– when the direct object or prepositional object of a sentence has the same reference as the subject.

> *John looked at **her**.*
> *John looked at **himself**.*
> *John taught **himself** to play the guitar.*

The reflexive form ***oneself*** can be used to refer to people in general.

> *The first golden rule is not to take **oneself** too seriously.*

It can also be used as a substitute for the 1st person singular. If it is used like this, the subject pronoun should be ***one***. In normal direct speech this usage is often felt to be rather pretentious.

> *One asks **oneself** whether it is worth the bother.*
> *One owes it to **oneself** to do something worthwhile.*

Some verbs take a reflexive pronoun only in particular uses of the verb.

> *Jeremy introduced **himself**.*
> *The cat washed **itself**.*

The reflexive pronoun can be left out if it is obvious that the subject was performing the action of the verb on him- or herself.

> *Jeremy **washed** and **dressed**, then went out.*

When a preposition is followed by a pronoun, the pronoun is normally in the object form.

> *They all looked at **him** in silence.*

If that pronoun refers to the subject of the main verb, however, it must be a reflexive pronoun.

> *She looked at **herself** in the mirror.*

- The reflexive can be used to make something you say stronger. To make a strong point, we sometimes use a normal subject or object pronoun and a reflexive pronoun as well.

  > *He told me **himself** that he was leaving.*
  > *I'll do it **myself**.*

- The reflexive can also be used with or without *by* meaning 'alone' or 'without help'.

  > *I think you should try and do it **yourself**.*
  > *Did she do that all by **herself**?*

The compound pronouns **each other** and **one another** are not true reflexives. They are used when two or more subjects mutually take part in an action. They are sometimes called **reciprocals**.

> They should stop blaming **one another**.
> We will always love **each other**.

Possessive pronouns

Possessive pronouns are used when you want to indicate who owns or is associated with an item.

> All those books are **hers**.
> Those suitcases are **ours**.
> Are you selling those books? I'd never sell any **of mine**.
> Those awful cousins **of yours** are here.
> This TV is really cheap. – Yes, **ours** was a bit more expensive, but better quality.

There are separate forms for the singular and the plural except in the 2nd person. In the 3rd person singular the form changes to match the gender of the possessor.

> I'm looking for Helen's trainers. Perhaps these are **hers**.
> These are our seats and the ones in front are **yours**.

possessive determiner	possessive pronoun
my	**mine**
your (singular)	**yours**
his	**his**
her	**hers**
its	(no form)
our	**ours**
your (plural)	**yours**
their	**theirs**

Note that none of these words should be spelled with an apostrophe. Avoid the common mistake of writing *it's* for the possessive form. *It's* is a short form for *it is*.

The demonstrative pronouns

The **demonstrative pronouns** are used instead of a noun phrase to indicate distance in time or space in relation to the speaker. They also indicate grammatical number – singular or plural.

	singular	*plural*
near	**this**	**these**
far	**that**	**those**

- Note that the demonstrative pronouns have the same spelling as demonstrative determiners. See also p. 160. Usually a demonstrative pronoun substitutes for a noun phrase that contains the same word being used as a determiner.

  Would you like to share some of this pizza with me?
  *Would you like to share **this** with me?*
  I'd like you to put these things away before we go.
  *I'd like you to put **these** away before we go.*

- It is regarded as impolite to use a demonstrative pronoun to refer directly to a person, except when making introductions.

  *John, **this** is Harry Forbes, my colleague.*
  ***This** is my husband, Rob.*
  *Mum, **this** is my form teacher, Miss Evans.*

Relative pronouns

The relative pronouns are the words *who*, *whom*, *which*, and *that*.

	person	*thing*
subject	**who** or **that**	**which** or **that**
object	**whom** or **that**	**which** or **that**
possessive	**whose**	**whose**

The function of a relative pronoun is to link a subordinate clause to a main clause.

> **He might lose his job,** *which would be disastrous.*
> *She promised* **to give away all the money,** *which was*
> *a bit rash.*

A subordinate clause introduced by a relative pronoun is called a **relative clause**.

Relative pronouns refer back to a noun phrase or pronoun that has just been mentioned. All relative pronouns must come as near as possible to the start of the clause that they are in. The only words that normally come before them in the clause are prepositions or conjunctions.

The choice of relative pronoun is influenced as follows:

– **That** as a relative pronoun never has a preposition before it.

> *That is* **a kind thought,** *for which I am most grateful.*
> *This is* **the person that** *Annie was talking about.*
> *This is* **the person about whom** *Annie was talking.*

– **Which** is not used for human subjects or objects.

> *That is* **the car** *which she has just bought.*
> *I have found* **a ring** *which you will love.*

– **Who** and **whom** are restricted to human subjects or objects.

> *He introduced me to* **his friend**, *who had just returned from China.*
> *I liked* **the actor** *who was playing Oedipus.*

– In **defining** relative clauses (see p. 270), **that** can be used instead of **which** and is sometimes used instead of **who** or **whom**.

> *I have found* **a ring** *which you will love.*
> *I have found* **a ring** *that you will love.*
> *She is* **the girl** *who was at Sam's party.*
> *She is* **the girl** *that was at Sam's party.*

The **object** form of the relative pronoun is used as the object of a verb or a preposition, but because **whom** is very formal, it is not often used: in everyday English, **who** is usually used instead.

> *The late* **Principal** *of the College,* **whom** *we all remember with affection, left this bursary in her will.*

> *I discovered* **who** *he was visiting.*   neutral
> *I discovered* **whom** *he was visiting.*   formal

• In informal writing and speech, any **preposition** is placed after the verb phrase instead of before the relative pronoun.

> *The girl* **who** *Brian was talking* **to** *seemed nervous.*
> *The people* **who** *he had been working* **for** *that summer had offered him a permanent job.*

- In informal and spoken English, a defining relative pronoun referring to the object of the clause may be left out entirely.

  *He is the **person** (that/who/whom) Annie was talking about.*
  *That is the **car** (which/that) she has just bought.*

Interrogative pronouns

The **interrogative pronouns** *who*, *whom*, and *whose* are used only for reference to people. The interrogative pronouns *which* and *what* are used for reference to things.

	subject	object	possessive
people	who	whom	whose
things	which what	which what	

Interrogative pronouns allow us to build a question around the thing that the pronoun refers to. See p. 237, where they are explained more generally under the heading of **WH-** words.

> **Who** *is dancing with Lucy?*
> **Which** *of these books would you recommend?*
> **What** *do you do when you're on holiday?*
> **Whose** *are these clothes?*

Who is used to ask questions about people in general.

> **Who** *is that man over there?*
> **Who** *did this?*
> **Who** *controls the day-to-day running of the business?*

What is used to ask questions about things in general when the answer is an open one. **What** can be either a subject or an object in a clause.

> **What** *happened next?*
> **What** *did you have for lunch?*

Which is used to ask for identification of a particular person or a particular thing in a group.

> **Which** *do you prefer, working in theatre or film?*
> **Which** *is your favourite Simpsons episode?*

Whose is the possessive form of the pronoun. It is used when a person is the possessor.

> **Whose** *is that sports car outside?*
> **Whose** *side are you on?*

- **Whom** is the object form of **who**. It is a very formal word and one which most speakers avoid using in casual conversation, when **who** could be used instead. When writing, however, it is usual to use **whom**.

  Informal
  Who *do you have in mind?*
  Who *were you speaking* **to**?

  Formal
  Whom *have you in mind?*
  To whom *were you speaking?*

- The object forms of the interrogative pronoun are used after a preposition. In informal and everyday usage, you can place the preposition at the end of the clause.

  Who *does this belong* **to**?   Informal
  To whom *does this belong?*   Formal

Indefinite pronouns

The indefinite pronouns are used when you do not know or do not need to say precisely who or what you are referring to. The noun phrase which they substitute for can refer to a person, a thing, or a group of people or things, in which gender and number are not made clear.

> **Someone** will have to tell her that she's failed.
> **Everybody** had a wonderful time.
> **Anything** is better than nothing.
> **Nothing** can make up for this loss.
> Some people like that sort of thing. **Others** don't.

The indefinite pronouns can be grouped according to meaning, as follows:

A General amounts and quantities: *most, some, none, any, all, both, half, several, enough, many, each.*

> **Many** find it impossible to cope.
> Congratulations from **all** at the club.
> Judging by the comments, **most** wanted her to stay on.
> Although we lost a lot of stuff in the fire, **some** was saved.
> **Enough** has been said on this topic to fill a book.

B Choice or alternatives: *either, neither.*

> Could you bring me one of those spanners? **Either** will do.
> **Neither** was keen on a traditional wedding.

C Undefined singular or multiple persons and things:

someone	somebody	something
no one	nobody	nothing
anyone	anybody	anything
everyone	everybody	everything

> Note the form of **no one** or, less usually, **no-one**.

- The pronouns in group C that refer to people can cause problems concerning the **number** and **gender** of a following determiner or pronoun. Traditionally, only the use of a following **singular** form was permitted. Common practice uses the plural form *their* and avoids awkward expressions like *his or her*.

> **Everybody** has **their** ups and downs.
> Has **anybody** finished **their** lunch yet?
> **No one** in **their** right mind goes on holiday there in January.

Many of these pronouns, especially those in groups A and B, have the same form as determiners. See p. 160.

- The way to tell them apart is to see if the word on its own is used as a subject, an object, or the complement of a verb; if it is, it is a **pronoun**. If, on the other hand, it is used in front of a noun, it is a **determiner**.

> As a pronoun:
> **Both** were given life sentences.
> **Several** managed to escape.
> I've found **some**!

> As a determiner:
> **Both men** were given life sentences.
> **Several sheep** managed to escape.
> I've found **some scrap paper**.

- The pronouns in Groups A and B are often used like partitives, with *of* and a noun phrase or a personal pronoun.

  None *of the children were hurt, but* **most** *of them were rather upset.*
  Neither *of his parents remarried.*

Prepositions

A preposition is one of a small but very common group of words that relate different items to each other. Most English prepositions have a number of meanings that are particular to each preposition.

Simple prepositions consist of one word, e.g. *in*, *on*, *under*. Complex prepositions consist of more than one word, e.g. *due to*, *together with*, *on top of*, *in spite of*, *out of*.

Prepositions enable us:

- to express movement to or from a **place**.
- to express **location** and **time**.

Prepositions are normally followed by:

- a noun phrase.

> in **time**   over **the edge**
> under **the table**   together with **my friends**

- an **-ing** clause.

> Thanks **for looking**.
> He picked up some extra cash **by working** in a bar at night.

- a relative pronoun (**WH-** word).

> He's married to Rachel, **with whom** he has one daughter.

In everyday speech a preposition may end a relative clause rather than come before it. See also p. 270.

> That's the girl we were talking **about**.
> That's the man (**who**) I gave the money **to**.

A preposition needs an object, rather like a transitive verb. A preposition and the noun phrase that goes with it is called a **prepositional phrase**.

A prepositional phrase is used as an **adverbial**.

> He put the flowers **on the table**.
> She shut the dog **in the kitchen**.
> He found the papers **in time for the meeting**.

or a **postmodifier**.

> **The house on the corner** has at last been sold.
> **The flowers on the table** are from Tim.
> **A bird with brilliant plumage** roamed the lawns.

* Prepositions combine with some verbs to make new meanings from the combination. These are one type of **phrasal verb**. See p. 81.

> I **believe in** his innocence.
> I **stand for** justice.
> She **went through** a bad patch.

The list below shows all the common simple prepositions. Some words can be either **prepositions** or **adverbs**, depending on how they are used and what they combine with. The words in *italics* are the prepositions that can also be used as **adverbs**.

> *aboard*, *about*, *above*, *across*, *after*, against, *along*, *alongside*, amid, among, *around*, as, at, atop, bar, *before*, *behind*, *below*, *beneath*, *beside*, *between*, *beyond*, *by*, despite, *down* during, for, from, *in*, *inside*, into, like, *near*, of, *off*, *on*, onto, *opposite*, *outside*, *over*, *past*, pending, per, prior, pro, re, regarding, *round*, *since*, than, *through*, *throughout*, till, to, towards, *under*, *underneath*, until, unto, *up*, upon, via, with, *within*, *without*.

The example below shows adverbial uses.

> He went **in**.
> I took it **through**.

When a verb is followed by a preposition, there is often little or no choice as to which preposition to use, e.g. *rely* **on**, *speak* **to**, *give* **to**.

When there is a choice of preposition, the meaning changes with each:

check **for**, *check* **on**, *check* **over**; *speak* **to**, *speak* **about**; *talk* **to**, *talk* **with**.

Prepositions allow us to express relationships. These are mostly to do with place and time. Some prepositions can be used with more than one meaning, depending on how we think about the time or place we are discussing.

Prepositions of location

Prepositions can indicate:

– the direction in which something is moving in relation to another person or thing: *towards, from, to, off*.

> They ran **towards** the station.
> He took the road **from** the town **to** the nearest village.

– something or someone being enclosed: *within, in, inside, outside*.

> The lake can be seen from most positions **within** the room.
> There seems to be something loose **inside** the control box.
> You have to stand **outside** the room while we make up some questions.
> Did you put the cheese back **in** the fridge?

– being at a certain point: *on, at, by, near*.

> Don't stand **on** the beds.
> I'll meet you **at** the library.
> There is a huge park **near** where I live.

– movement over or onto a place: *over, across, on, onto*.

> Graham jumped **onto** the back of the lorry.
> He slid the packet **across** the table.
> Warms tears flowed **over** his cheeks.

– location as a line: *along, over, on*.

> We walked **along** the bank of the river.
> Please sign **on** the dotted line.

Prepositions of time

Prepositions can also indicate:

– a point in time or a date : *at, on, in*.

> The baby arrived **at** 9 p.m. **on** April 1st.
> They got married **in** June.
> I'll be with you **in** five minutes.

– a period or point of time which marks a change: *before, after, since, until*.

> We lived there **before** Mother died.
> I went to that school **until** I was sixteen.
> I usually go there **after** work.

– the duration of some event: *for*.

> Helen stayed there **for** the whole of July.

Word order in sentences

The order of words in an English sentence is very important. A change in word order often results in a change of meaning.

Many other languages use **inflection**, a change in the form of words, to show how the parts of a sentence function. English has very few inflections, so the place that a word occupies in a sentence, its **syntax**, is the most important feature.

Neutral word order

Most sentences have a subject, and then something that is said about the subject, which is usually the rest of the sentence. This divides the sentence into the **subject** and the **predicate**.

> *John* (subject) *bought the tickets on Saturday* (predicate).
> *The wall* (subject) *was torn down* (predicate).
> *My elderly mother* (subject) *is rather deaf* (predicate).

Most sentences put the information that they carry in this order. This is neutral word order. When this neutral order is changed, the meaning of a sentence also changes.

> *The **cat** killed the dog.*
> *The **dog** killed the cat.*
> *The **child** watched the rabbit.*
> *The **rabbit** watched the child.*

Word order in simple sentences

Simple sentences are those which have only one clause. They are extremely common in all forms of written and spoken English. Simple sentences have a normal word order which varies according to whether the sentence is:

– a **statement**,

> I *saw you* at the theatre on Saturday night.
> I *didn't see you* at the theatre on Saturday night.

– a **question**,

> *Did I see you* at the theatre on Saturday night?
> *Didn't I see you* at the theatre on Saturday night?

– a **command**.

> You *should buy* a ticket now.
> You *shouldn't buy* a ticket yet.
> *Buy* a ticket now.
> *Don't buy* a ticket now.

Word order also varies according to whether the sentence is **negative** or **positive**.

Focusing

When we want to focus the attention of a reader or a listener on a particular word or phrase, we can use variations on neutral order, such as putting the subject last, splitting the clause into two, or repeating some part of the sentence.

Some variations on the theme of neutral word order.

> We used to call him 'Fuzzy'.
> 'Fuzzy', we used to call him.
> Didn't we use to call him 'Fuzzy'?
> 'Fuzzy' was what we used to call him.
> It was 'Fuzzy' we used to call him.

Declarative, interrogative, and imperative statements

Each sentence in English provides some type of information. For example, a sentence can be a statement, a question, a request, a command, a denial or a response, etc. In English the choice and order of the parts of a sentence help us express these meanings.

Most statements and denials are in the **declarative**. An important feature of declarative sentences is that they have a subject that comes before the verb.

> Our dog **eats** any old thing.
> Our dog **won't** just **eat** any old thing.
> The dog **has** already **been fed**.
> The dog **hasn't been fed** yet.
> We **have** already **won** several races.
> We **haven't won** any races yet.

Most questions are in the **interrogative**. An important feature of interrogative sentences is that they normally have a subject that comes after an auxiliary verb.

> **Does** your dog **eat** any old thing?
> **Has** the dog already **been fed**?
> **Hasn't** the dog **been fed** yet?
> **Have** you **won** any races yet?
> **Haven't** you **won** any races yet?

If the subject does come first it will be a special question word.

> **Who won** the race?
> **Which** team **was** it?

- Exceptionally, we can ask questions using the declarative. We do this by using a special tone of voice.

You're telling me he has a new car? I don't believe it.
It's raining again? That makes three days running.

Many commands are in the **imperative**. Commands in the imperative have no word that acts as a subject, though the subject is understood to be *you*. Commands in the imperative can sometimes sound rude or impatient.

Eat up quickly. We have to go!
Leave me alone.
On your marks, get set ... go!

- We can make a **request**, which is a type of command, sound more polite by using the interrogative.

Would you feed the dog, please.
Would you mind shutting the door.
Could I have that now, thank you.

> Not all imperative sentences are orders or commands. They can be social expressions.
>
> *Have a nice day.*
> *Get well soon.*
> *Help yourselves to coffee.*

There is also a **subjunctive** form. This is rarely used in English now. It may be used when you want to talk about an improbable or unlikely situation.

If I were Prime Minister, I'd spend more money on education.

The declarative

The **declarative** is used to make statements. A statement is usually the expression of a fact or of an opinion. Statements can be both positive or negative.

> *Kate is not working after all.*
> *Tim wasn't reading your diary.*
> *Helen wasn't talking about you.*
> *I'm not going on holiday this year.*

Declarative sentences always contain a subject and a following verb phrase.

The normal word order for declarative sentences:

subject + verb phrase

> *Kate is working.*
> *Tim was reading.*
> *Helen stared at me in surprise.*

subject + verb phrase + direct object

> *Ross is writing a letter.*
> *Pam borrowed three library books.*
> *Stephen ordered vegetarian lasagne.*

subject + verb phrase + adverbial

> *Dominic was eating very slowly.*
> *Lyndsey was studying in her room.*
> *Mikhail laughed nervously.*

subject + verb phrase + direct object + adverbial

> *Dominic was eating his lunch very slowly.*
> *Lyndsey had been reading a book in her room.*

Certain verbs must have following objects, e.g. *see, find, prefer, take.*

> *She saw **her friend**.*
> *He found **a camera**.*
> *They took **a holiday brochure**.*

Other verbs need, or can have, both a **direct** and an **indirect** object, e.g. *give, buy, offer.*

> *Laura offered **me another biscuit**.*
> *Scott's uncle bought **him a new bike**.*

The word order can be either:

subject + verb + indirect object + direct object

> *Kate gave **the dog a bone**.*
> *Stuart bought **Marie a birthday present**.*

or, with the addition of a word that indicates the recipient:

subject + verb + direct object + to/for + indirect object.

> *Kate gave **a bone to the dog**.*
> *Stuart bought **a birthday present for Marie**.*

Another group of verbs must be followed either by an object and an adverbial expression, or an adverbial expression on its own e.g. *put, place, stand*.

> Richard placed **the computer** on the table.
> Diana put **her jeans** in the drawer.
> Michael stood **in the middle of the pitch**.

A further type of declarative statement has the same basic order of subject and verb as the **subject + verb phrase + direct object** example on p. 227, but with a **complement** replacing the direct object. See p. 230 for more about complements and p. 11 for more about objects.

> Elisabeth seems to have been **rather worried** lately.
> This dessert is **delicious**.

Complements

Some verbs such as *be, become, seem,* do not have an object but a
complement.

The **subject complement** is a word or phrase that tells us more about
the subject.

> Alan is ***a nice person***.
> Rajiv is ***a psychiatric nurse***.
> Alison seems ***very well balanced***.
> Rosamund is ***herself*** again.
> That's ***it***!
> This is for ***you***.

The subject complement is linked to the subject by a verb, and the
order is as follows:

subject + verb + subject complement

Subject complements may be either noun phrases, pronouns,
adjectives, or even prepositional phrases.

* Most adjectives can be used after a group of verbs that includes:
  appear, be, become, look, seem, smell, taste, etc. An adjective that
  is used in this position is called a **predicative** adjective and it is
  functioning as a **complement**.

> The tickets seemed ***expensive***, but the show was ***excellent***.
> These little cakes are ***delicious***.
> Soon afterwards, Patrick became ***ill***.
> Jackie appeared ***friendly enough*** when I first met her.

Less frequently we find an **object complement**. The object complement
tells us more about the direct object. It relates directly to the object
and is placed after it.

Verbs that can take an object complement with their direct object include *make*, *call*, and *appoint*. The word order is as follows:

subject + verb + direct object + object complement

> *Peter's phone call made* **Maureen** **happy**.
> *She called* **me** **a fool**.
> *They appointed* **him** **Director**.

Word order in negative statements

In negative statements, the basic word order for subject and object is the same as in positive statements.

> *John has gone to school.*
> *John has **not** gone to school.*

The difference is that negative statements must contain **not**, and must have as part of the verb phrase, either:

– a **primary auxiliary** verb,

> *She **had not** arrived in time for lunch.*
> *Kate **is not** working this evening.*
> *Tim **was not** reading your diary.*

– one or other of the **modal auxiliary** verbs, or

> *I warn you, he **may not** want to come.*
> *Ailsa **could not** see the road clearly.*

– a form of **be** used as a main verb.

> *That **is not** my book.*

The word **not** is added immediately after the first one of these auxiliary verbs. The main verb follows.

The word order is, therefore:
   subject + **auxiliary** + **not** + **main verb.**

A negative sentence may contain a modal verb and one or more auxiliaries as well.

> I **may not have** gone *by the time you arrive.*
> They **could not have** seen *her – they were asleep in bed.*
> They **should not have been playing** *in the road.*

In this case the word order is:
   subject + **modal** + *not* + **primary auxiliary** + **main verb**.

If the verb phrase does not already contain one of these verbs, then it is necessary to add the **supporting auxiliary** verb *do*.

The present simple and the past simple tenses of main verbs take the appropriate form of *do*, and then add *not* followed by the base form of the main verb.

> *He runs.*
> *He* **does not** *run.*
> *He ran.*
> *He* **did not** *run.*
> *Lynn* **does not** *work overtime now.*
> *The bus service* **did not** *run on Sundays.*

The word order is, therefore:
   subject + *do-* **auxiliary** + *not* + **main verb**

See p. 235 for more on the supporting auxiliary.

• The contracted form of **not**, which is **n't**, can be used after every auxiliary verb except *am*. This is the most common spoken form.

> *He* **doesn't** *run.*
> *He* **didn't** *run.*
> *Lynn* **doesn't** *work on Sundays.*
> *She* **hasn't** *been to work all week.*
> *He* **isn't** *going to come after all.*
> *Bill went swimming but Ann* **didn't** *fancy it.*

The full form with **not** tends to be used more in writing.

> **can** + **not** is usually written **cannot**.
>
> She **can't** come.
> She **cannot** come.

- Other words with a negative meaning, **never**, **barely**, **hardly**, **scarcely**, **rarely**, do not change the order of words in a statement.

  She **doesn't buy** Vogue.
  She **never buys** Vogue.
  He **barely** earns enough to live on.
  I **hardly** think that is going to put them off.

The interrogative

The interrogative is normal for many questions. It contains a verb phrase that is followed by a subject.

There are two main types of question: those that can be answered *yes* or *no*, and those that have to be answered with a specific piece of information or a sentence such as *I don't know*. Each type of question has its own special word order.

Yes/no questions

Questions that expect the answer *yes* or *no* are called **yes/no questions** or sometimes, **polar questions**.

The **interrogative** is used to form yes/no questions.

The normal sentence order for the interrogative is:
   modal/auxiliary verb + **subject** + **base form** of the **main verb**.

> ***Were*** *the dogs barking?*
> ***Have*** *you been dieting?*
> ***Can*** *Mahmoud come too?*
> ***Must*** *you go so soon?*
> ***Would*** *you like a chocolate?*

When a sentence does not contain a modal verb or an auxiliary verb, the question is formed by placing a form of the supporting auxiliary verb *do* before the subject and following it with the **base form** of the main verb.

> ***Does*** *he enjoy tennis?*
> ***Do they*** *play a lot?*
> ***Did*** *that surprise his mum?*

Yes/no questions also have a negative form. **Negative yes/no questions** are almost always contracted. The negative in its contracted form *n't* comes immediately before the subject.

> **Doesn't** *he like talking about his childhood?*
> **Can't** *Peter have one too?*
> **Don't** *you speak French?*
> **Wouldn't** *you like to know a bit more about this?*

If the full negative form *not* is used, it comes immediately after the subject. The full form is very formal.

> **Does** *he* **not** *like talking about his childhood?*
> **Do** *you* **not** *want to know what it was about?*
> **Can** *Peter* **not** *have one too?*

WH- questions

When you want to get a detailed answer, not just *yes* or *no*, you must use a **WH- question** (or **'non-polar' question**), which allows for many possible answers. The words **who**, **whom**, **whose**, **what**, **which**, **when**, **where**, **why**, and **how** are used to form this sort of question. These words are referred to as **WH-** words. See pp. 237–240.

> **Yes/no:**
> **Did you ring** *the school? – Yes, I did.*
> **Was she** *all right in the end? – No/I don't know.*
> **Have you seen** *Ali yet? – Yes, I have.*

> **WH-:**
> **Who** *was that man? – He's my geography teacher.*
> **What** *did he say when you told him the news? – He was too surprised to say anything.*
> **When** *did you see Ali? – Last Wednesday.*
> **Where** *is Peter going? – To work.*
> **When** *did they arrive? – Yesterday.*
> **Why** *have you stopped going running? – The doctor told me to.*

WH- words

The **WH-** words are also called **interrogatives**. They are used for **WH-** questions. They can be determiners, adverbs, or pronouns.

WH- determiners

When used as determiners, *what*, *which*, or *whose* can be used to ask questions:

– about nouns

> *What book are you reading?*
> *Which plane is he catching?*
> *Whose jacket is this?*

– or about the pronoun *one* or *ones*.

> *Which one would you like?*
> *Which ones did Ruth want?*

- The determiner *which* can be used in questions about selecting. It can also be used together with the preposition *of* for the same purpose.

> *Which colour shall we use?*
> *Which book sells the most copies?*
> *Which of these colours shall we use?*
> *Of all your novels, which of them did you enjoy writing the most?*

- The determiner *whose* asks about possession with reference to a person as the possessor.

> *Whose mother did you say she was?*
> *Whose bag is this?*

WH- adverbs

The adverb **WH-** words, **when**, **where**, **how**, and **why**, always make the sentence follow the interrogative word order.

– **When** asks about time.

> **When** will they arrive?
> **When** shall I see you again?

– **Where** asks about place.

> **Where** are you going?
> **Where** have you been?
> **Where** is your coat?

– **How** asks about manner.

> **How** did you get here? – We came by train.
> **How** does this thing work?

– **Why** asks about reasons and purpose. Questions with **why** are usually answered with a clause containing *because* to express reason, or with the *to* infinitive to express purpose.

> **Why** is the baby crying? – **Because** she's hungry.
> **Why** are you saving your money? – **To buy** a bike.

– **How much** implies reference to a quantity; **how many** implies reference to an amount or a countable number of things but may leave out the noun referred to.

> **How much** money did they take? – All of it.
> **How much** does it cost? – £4.20.
> **How many** packs do you want? – Twelve, please.
> **How many** do you want? – Twelve, please.

– **How** can also be used with adjectives such as *old*, *big*, *far*, or with adverbs such as *often*, *soon*, *quickly* to ask about degree, rate, or timing.

> **How far** is it to the station? – About five kilometres.
> **How often** does he come? – Not very often.

WH- pronouns

The **pronouns who**, **whose**, **which**, and **what** can be the subject or object of a verb.

> **Who** can help me?
> **Whose** is the new sports car outside?
> **Which** was your best subject at school?
> **What** happened next?
> **What** have you got to take with you to camp?

The interrogative pronoun **whose** is used when the question is asked about a person as the possessor of something. See also pp. 201–202 on interrogative and relative pronouns.

> **Whose** is the motorbike parked outside?
> **Whose** is this?

• The form **whom** is used as the object of a verb or of a preposition in very formal or old-fashioned English.

> **Whom** did you talk to?
> **Whom** would you rather have as a boss?

Modern English usage prefers **who** instead of **whom** in all but the most formal contexts.

> **Who** did you talk to?
> **Who** would you rather have as a boss?

When **whom** is used as the object of a preposition, it normally follows the preposition.

> **To whom** *did you speak?*
> **With whom** *did she go?*

When **who** is used, the preposition is placed at the end of the clause.

> **Who** *did you speak* **to**?
> **Who** *did she go* **with**?

The **WH-** subject pronouns are found in the same sentence order as statements:
WH- subject pronoun + the main verb.

> **Who can help** *me?*
> **Whose is** *that motorbike parked outside?*
> **Which was** *your best subject at school?*
> **What happened** *next?*

The **WH-** object pronouns make the sentence take the word order of a question:
WH- object pronoun + primary or modal auxiliary + subject + base form of the verb.

> **What** *do you have* to take *with you to camp?*
> **What** *has Jonathan done* *now?*

- The exception to this is in informal spoken English, when the speaker wants to show shock or disbelief.

> *You did* **what**?

Sentence tags

Tags are short additions that look like questions, used at the end of a declarative sentence. They are sometimes called **question tags**, but many sentences ending with a tag are not real questions. They are usually used to check that the listener agrees with what the speaker has said. Sentence tags are very commonly used in spoken English, but not in formal written English.

The tag is added to the end of a statement. If the auxiliary verb *be* or *have* or a **modal** verb is part of the verb phrase in the sentence, then it is used as the verb in the sentence tag.

> It **isn't** raining again, **is it**?
> You**'ve seen** the programme, **haven't you**?
> Well, we **can't jump** over it, **can we**?
> You **will come**, **won't you**?

If the main verb is in the present simple or past simple tense, the tag is made using *do*.

> He certainly **likes** eating, **doesn't he**?
> I **slipped up** there, **didn't I**?

In negative tags, *n't* is added to the auxiliary. Note that this contracted form is always used.

> He certainly **likes** eating, **doesn't he**?
> I **slipped up** there, **didn't I**?
> They **went** with you, **didn't they**?

- The formal forms such as, *does he not*, *did I not*, *have you not*, sound old-fashioned. They are more common in some regional varieties of English.

The pronoun in the sentence tag must match the subject of the main verb.

> **You** *aren't listening, are* **you**?
> **He** *reads a lot, doesn't* **he**?

Sentence tags can be **negative**

> *They* **went** *with you,* **didn't they**?

or **positive**.

> *Your father* **doesn't belong to** *the golf club,* **does he**?

Normally, when the first part of the sentence is positive, the tag verb will be negative, and vice versa. Sentences in which both parts are positive are less common. These sentences must be used carefully as, with certain tones of voice, they can sound aggressive or judgemental.

> *I see, you* **think** *I'm a fool,* **do** *you?*
> *So you* **smoke** *now,* **do** *you?*

- The same sentence tag may have different meanings depending on the tone of voice that is used with it.

> Falling tone: statement
> *She's gone out, hasn't she?*

> Rising tone: question
> *She's gone out, hasn't she?*

The sentence can be a statement of fact or a question, depending on whether your voice rises or falls at the end. However, a question mark is always required.

Sentence tags are used in the following combinations:

- To say something that the speaker expects the listener will agree with. This doesn't always sound like a question:

positive main verb + **negative tag**

> Mary **will pass** her driving test this time, **won't she**?
> Richard **seems** to have lost interest in everything, **doesn't he**?

or **negative main verb** + **positive tag**

> Jessica **didn't care**, **did she**?
> Kerry **hadn't done** enough preparation, **had she**?

- To point out or remark on something, often something that the listener cannot deny. This frequently sounds more like a question:

positive main verb + **negative tag**

> You've just **bought** a new car, **haven't you**?
> Henry **has been** away already this year, **hasn't he**?

or **negative main verb** + **positive tag**

> Desmond **hasn't been** to see you, **has he**?
> Paula **wasn't** in your class at school, **was she**?

- To show interest in something. This often repeats part of what the previous speaker has said:

positive main verb + **positive tag**

> You **saw** him in town, **did you**?
> So, you **come** from New Zealand, **do you**?
> So you've just **come back** from skiing, **have you**?

When a tag is used to show interest in something, the sentence is often begun with *So*. This type of tag can also be used in a challenging manner.

> *Oh, so you**'ve been here** all the time, **have you**?*

After a command, a tag made with *can, could, will, shall,* or *would* makes an order more polite.

> *Make me a cup of tea, **will you**?*
> *Just wait a minute, **would you**?*
> *Let's go to the cinema, **shall we**?*

The imperative

Commands and orders

The **imperative** is used to give commands and orders. The form of the verb used for the imperative is the **base form** of the main verb, which is used without a subject.

> ***Walk*** *to the corner,* ***turn*** *right, and* ***cross*** *the road.*
> ***Open*** *your mouth and* ***say*** *'Aaaah'.*

- Although the main feature of sentences in the imperative is that they have no **grammatical** subject, they do have an **understood** subject, '*you*'.

The basic form of the imperative remains the same whether it is addressed to one or more people.

> *Come on,* ***Mary****; I'm waiting.*
> *Come on,* ***girls****; you're late.*

There is also a special type of imperative, using ***let's***, that is used when you need to include the speaker. See p. 247.

The word order of a sentence in the imperative is:
   verb + **object** (if needed).

The negative imperative is made with ***do*** + ***not*** or ***don't***.

> ***Don't lose*** *that key.*
> ***Do not come back*** *without it!*

The uses of the imperative are as follows:

– to give an order.

> *Go* away.
> *Stop* that.
> *Keep* quiet.

– to give instructions.

> *Don't use* this spray near a naked flame.
> *Apply* the glue thinly and *leave* it for ten minutes.

– to give advice or warnings.

> *Don't forget* to take your passport with you.
> *Be* careful!
> *Don't go* on the ice.

– to make an offer or an invitation.

> *Have* a piece of cake.
> *Come* round and *see* me some time.

The imperative of *do* + a **main verb** can be used:

– for polite emphasis.

> *Do take* your coat off.

– to be persuasive.

> *Do try* to eat a little of this; it will be good for you.

– to show irritation.

> **Do stop** talking! I'm trying to work.

• Note that the imperative is not the only way to form a command or an order. You can also issue a command when you use a sentence in the declarative or the interrogative.

> I'm certainly not going to get it – **you get it**.
> **Would you get it**, then? I'm busy.

Making suggestions

Let's (**let** + **us**) + **main verb** is used in the 1st person plural only, especially when you are trying to encourage someone to do something with you.

It includes both the speaker and the hearer, so the subject that is understood is represented by the plural *we*.

> **Let's visit** Malcolm this weekend.
> **Please let's go** to the cinema tonight.
> **Do let's have** a look at your new computer, Chris.
> **Let's pool** our resources.

• Suggestions which start with **let's** often end with the sentence tag **shall we**?

> **Let's phone** her now, **shall we**?
> **Let's go** for a walk after supper, **shall we**?

In ordinary English the negative is **let's not** + **main verb** or sometimes **don't let's** + **main verb**.

> **Let's not worry** about that now.
> **Don't let's worry** about that now.

In formal English, the negative is **let us not** + **main verb**.

> **Let us not lose** sight of our aims.

Do let's is the emphatic form.

> It's a very good bargain; **do let's buy** it!

- The uncontracted form **let us** + **main verb** is occasionally used in formal and written English.

> **Let us be** clear about this.
> **Let us** hope that this will never happen again.

The answer to a suggestion with **let's** is normally either, yes, let's or no, let's not or sometimes, no, don't let's (...).

> **Let's phone** her now, shall we? – **Yes, let's**.
> **Let's phone** her now, shall we? – **No, let's not**.
> **Let's invite** Malcolm over this weekend. – No, **don't let's** do that.

The vocative

The imperative is often used with a **vocative**. This is where you mention a person's name or some other way of identifying the person to whom a command or request is being addressed.

> **David**, *come here!*
> *Come here,* **David**.
> *Hey,* **you**, *stop talking!*

The vocative can be a proper noun, the pronoun *you*, or a noun phrase. The vocative can come before or after the main clause. A vocative forms a part of many questions.

> **Peter**, *do you know where I put the DVD?*
> *Have you seen Chris recently,* **Jenny**?

A vocative is also combined with an interrogative clause to form a request.

> **Tony**, *would you pass me the hammer?*
> *Could I speak to you privately for a minute,* **Sue**?

When a vocative is used with an imperative clause, the sentence is usually a command.

> **Sam**, *get off there!*
> **You**, *come back!*

A command can also be phrased as a request.

> **Would you stop** *talking now, darling, and go to sleep.*
> **Would you get** *off there, please, Sam.*

A practical reason for using a vocative is to supply the missing but understood subject, so that the right person will understand the command or request, and act on it.

Note the punctuation. There should be a comma between the vocative part of the clause and the remainder.

As part of a command, except for urgent warnings, the use of the vocative is considered rude or abrupt.

The subjunctive

The **subjunctive** was formerly used in English for situations that were improbable or that expressed a wish. It is only rarely used in modern British English. It is, however, found in certain set phrases and in very formal forms of speech and writing.

> God **save** the Queen!
> God **bless** you!
> God **help** us!
> Heaven **help** us!
> Heaven **forbid** that that should happen to me.
> **Suffice** it to say he escaped with only a caution.

The present subjunctive

The form in the present tense is exactly the same as the base form in all persons of the verb. That is, there is no **-s** on the 3rd person singular.

The subjunctive is used, in very formal English, in subordinate clauses that follow verbs expressing a desire, a demand, a formal recommendation, or a resolve.

> I only ask that he **cease** behaving in this extraordinary manner.
> It is vital that they **be** stopped at once.
> Is it really necessary that she **work** all hours of the day?
> I demand that he **do** something to make up for this.

The clause containing the subjunctive is linked to the main clause with *that*.

- This use of the subjunctive is more common in American English than in British English. British speakers usually take advantage of other ways of expressing the same message, especially in less formal speech.

> *I only ask that **he should cease** behaving in this extraordinary manner.*
> *It is vital that they **are** stopped at once.*
> *It is vital **to stop** them at once.*
> *Is it really necessary **for her to work** all hours of the day?*
> *I demand that **he does** something to make up for this.*

The past subjunctive

In written English and in very formal speech, the past subjunctive form **were** is sometimes used with the 1st and 3rd person singular, in place of the normal past form **was**.

The past subjunctive may be used:

– after *if* or *I wish*, to express regret or longing

> *If your father **were** alive he would help you.*
> *If I **were** rich I would buy a Ferrari.*
> *I wish I **were** taller.*
> *If only he **were** here now!*

– after *as if/as though* and similar expressions, to express doubt or improbability.

> *You talk to him as if he **were** your slave!*
> *Some people behave as though dogs **were** human.*

Many people prefer to use the normal form of the past in this type of sentence. This is quite acceptable in ordinary English.

> If your father **was** alive he would help you.
> If I **was** rich I would buy a Ferrari.
> I wish I **was** tall.
> If only he **was** here now!
> You talk to him as if he **was** your slave!

Exclamations

Exclamations are short utterances that you make when you are very surprised or upset. They are not always whole sentences. Sometimes they are more like a noise than a word. In this case they are called **interjections**.

> *Ugh!*   *Phew!*
> *Wow!*   *Huh!*

Many exclamations consist of just one word.

> *Help!*   *Nonsense!*
> *Blast!*   *Rubbish!*

Exclamations can also consist of:

– *what* + **noun phrase**

> **What** *a pity!*
> **What** *a lovely day!*
> **What** *rubbish!*

– or *how* + **adjective**.

> **How** *silly!*
> **How** *kind of him!*

They may also have the form of a negative question.

> **Isn't** *it a warm day!*
> **Aren't** *they kind!*

- Another form of exclamation is when the hearer repeats part of the sentence that he or she has just heard. This is used when the hearer finds it hard to believe what has been said or is very surprised. This sort of exclamation is called an **echo**.

  *Richard's passed the exam. – **Richard's passed**! That's brilliant!*
  *Sally's here. – **She's here!** What a relief!*

Responses

Responses are made in answer to a question or a statement by another person in the course of conversation. Like exclamations, they may be full sentences, but can also be phrases or single words.

> *Yes.*
> *On Tuesday.*
> *I certainly will.*

Responses usually do not make sense on their own.

Although a response may not have a subject or contain a main verb, it can be classed as a sentence, because a response uses our knowledge of what has just been said. The subject or the verb will usually be understood from the context.

> *Are you coming to the party tonight?* – **Yes**.
> *When are you going to London, then?* – **On Tuesday**.
> *Will you be doing some shopping?* – **I certainly will**.

• If the verb is in a simple tense you can use the supporting auxiliary *do* as the verb in the response.

> *Do you like courgettes?* – *Yes, I **do***.

• You usually just use the first part of the verb phrase in a compound verb to make a response. That is, the first **auxiliary** verb or the **modal verb** becomes the response form.

> *Has Tamsin called round yet?* – *Yes, she **has***.
> *Was Andrea crying?* – *Yes, she **was***.
> *Can we leave early?* – *Yes, you **can***.
> *Should I be doing this differently?* – *Yes, you **should***.

Some speakers prefer to use the modal and the auxiliary form together.

> *Laurence could be running if it wasn't for his injury.*
> – *Yes, he **could be**.*

Sentences and clauses

A clause is a group of words which contains a verb. The verb in a clause can be finite

> **Use** this pan for the pasta.
> He **missed** the turnoff.

or non-finite.

> **To cook** pasta, always use a large pan.
> **Dreaming** about Jenny, he missed the turnoff.

Simple sentences

Simple sentences consist of one clause, in which the verb is finite.

> Ann **went** to the bank.
> She **withdrew** £100.

Two or more clauses can be joined to make a **compound** sentence or a **complex** sentence.

Complex sentences

Complex sentences are those that contain a **subordinate** clause as well as a **main** clause.

> **When he arrives, I'll phone you**.
> **He stayed at home because he felt ill**.

A **subordinate** clause is one that contains special information about the main clause. It will usually be introduced by a **linking word** such as when, if, because, or that. The linking words are called **subordinating conjunctions**.

Most subordinate clauses can come before, after, or within the main clause. Usually, when one clause is of principal importance and the other clause gives information about the principal one, we have a complex sentence with one **main clause** and one **subordinate clause**.

- The position that a subordinate clause is placed in is determined largely by what is felt to be the main message of a sentence.

> *Since you seem to have made up your mind, I'll say no more.*
> *I stopped seeing her because she moved to Liverpool.*

Compound sentences

A compound sentence is one that consists of two **main clauses**, joined by a word such as *and*, *but*, or *or*, called a **coordinating conjunction**. Each clause is of equal importance and gives information of equal value. The order of the clauses can be very important for the meaning. For example, the timing of an action can be described by the order in which the clauses follow each other.

> *He picked it up **and** ran over to her.*
> *He ran over to her **and** picked it up.*
> *I drove to Coatbridge **and** went on to Stirling.*

Compound-complex sentences

These have more than one main clause and at least one subordinate clause.

> *Angie came over **and** we decided to use my car **because** hers was playing up.*
> *He ran over to Julie, **who** was sitting at the end of the bench, **and** grabbed her handbag.*

Joining clauses

Coordination

The process called **coordination** joins two short clauses of equal importance with a conjunction. Each clause becomes a **main** clause in the new sentence.

> *Ann went to the bank **and** withdrew £100.*
> *Sally goes to work **but** Ann doesn't have a job.*
> *Ann (**either**) stays at home **or** visits her family.*

The clauses are linked by words called **coordinating conjunctions**, such as *and, but, (either) or, neither, nor,* or *yet*. Conjunctions come at the beginning of a clause.

- If the subject of both clauses is the same, it does not have to be repeated in front of the second verb.

> *She came over **and** ~~she~~ gave me a hug.*

The conjunction **and** is used:

- to join clauses where there is no contrast or choice.

- to join more than two clauses; the earlier clauses can be joined by a comma, but the last two must be joined by **and**.

> *Ann got into the car, drove to the bank, withdrew £100,*
> *   **and** went shopping.*

The conjunction **but** is used to join clauses where there is a contrast.

> *She wanted to buy a new dress **but** she couldn't find one she liked.*

The conjunction **yet** is used, mainly in written English, to join clauses where there is a contrast that is of a surprising nature.

> *He's a quietly spoken man,* **yet** *he still manages to command attention.*
> *She was suffering from a knee injury* **yet** *she still won the match.*

- The conjunctions *and, but, or, neither,* and *nor* are also used to join two phrases of the same kind,

> *This book is useful for* **planning and carrying out** *research.*
> **The former President and his wife** *were there.*

or two words of the same class.

> *I use this chair when I am* **reading and working**.
> *Do you undertake* **detailed or intricate** *work?*
> **Jack and Jill** *fell down the hill.*
> *This is a* **complicated but intriguing** *film.*

In particular, *and* and *but* are used to coordinate pairs of adjectives in a predicative position.

When there is a positive choice between the subjects of two clauses, you use the pair of words **either** and **or** to join the clauses.

> **Either** *you come to my place* **or** *I'll meet you at work. Which do you prefer?*

If the subject of the joined clauses is the same, the subject is used in the first of the joined clauses only. This is often also true of any auxiliary verbs that may be present.

> *Martin said he would* **either** *meet them for lunch* **or** *take them to tea.*

When it is used in this way *either* must come in one of these places:

- before the subject in the first clause of the group.
- in front of the main verb and after any auxiliary verb.

You can use *either...or* to join more than two clauses. *Or* is mandatory at the beginning of the final clause, and optional at the beginning of the previous clause.

> *Colin said he would (**either**) meet them for lunch,*
> *(**or**) take them to tea, **or** have them over for a coffee.*
> *Ian can (**either**) come with us **or** take a taxi later.*

The use of *either...or* emphasizes that the two clauses are alternatives and cannot both be true. Compare *and/or*.

> *Colin said he would meet them for lunch, **and/or** have them*
> *over for a coffee.*

The word *either* can be left out if the sentence meaning is clear. Some writers treat all but the final *or* as optional.

> You can use *or* on its own to join two or more clauses,
> but *either* cannot be used on its own.

When there is a negative choice between the subjects of two clauses, you can use the pair of words *neither* and *nor* to join the clauses.

> *It is **neither** possible **nor** desirable that they should be invited.*
> *Jane was **not** a fool; **neither/nor was she** prepared to be blamed*
> *for the error.*

The word *neither* can be used on its own to connect two clauses if the first clause contains a word with broad negative meaning such as *not*, *barely* or *scarcely*. If there is a subject in the second clause, question order must be used.

> There was **barely** enough meat for the children; **neither did they** have any bread.
> Eric **hardly** saw the fight; **nor did he** remember much about the incident later.

- The words **either** and **neither** can also be used as a pronoun or as a determiner. Each can then be used on its own; it does not then have a joining function.

> **Either** book will do. It doesn't matter.
> **Neither** book is at all suitable, I'm sorry.
> You can have **either**.

- **Either**, **or**, **neither**, and **nor** can be used as conjunctions inside a noun phrase or a verb phrase.

> You can choose to study **either Shakespeare or Keats**.
> **Neither Vimala nor Katie** knew the answer.
> She is **either desperate or just silly**.
> He didn't know whether **to stay or go**.

Subordination

When two or more clauses are joined by a conjunction other than *and*, *but*, *or*, or *yet*, one of the clauses is the main clause; the other clauses are **subordinate** clauses. The different types of subordinate clause include **noun** clauses,

> What matters most is **that you treat everyone fairly**.

adverbial clauses,

> They went outside **as soon as the rain stopped**.

relative clauses,

> This is the problem **that we're facing** at the moment.
> We stayed in Inverness, **which is in the Scottish Highlands**.

conditional clauses,

> Maureen plans to live in Australia **if she can get a job there**.

and **reported** clauses.

> She told me **that Philip was in France**.

Each of the subordinate clauses is associated with an introductory word that signals what type of clause it is that follows.

> **After** she had read the diary, she returned it to the drawer.
> **As** they were going downstairs, the phone rang.
> They aren't coming **because** they've had an argument.

These words are called **subordinating conjunctions**. They include:

– the **WH-** words

– words like *since, if, when, because*

– the word *that*, either on its own or used with another word
  e.g. *so that* or *supposing that*

– a phrase ending in *as*, e.g. *as soon as, as long as*

- Each of the subordinating clauses has a preferred position. For example, most adverbial clauses usually follow the main clause, although they can also come before the main clause.

> Shall I do the shopping **when I finish work**?
> **When I finish work**, I could do the shopping for you.

Reported clauses usually follow directly on from the main reporting clause. See p. 277.

Noun clauses

These are clauses that can be used as either the subject or the object of a sentence or in other places where a noun phrase is usually found. They are introduced by *that*

> What I like about him is **that he always tries his best**.

or by a **WH-** word, e.g. *who, when, where*.

> I don't know **where you live**.
> **How the thief got in** is a mystery.
> **Why she acts like this** is beyond me.

Word order after a **WH-** word is the same as in a statement.

> The subordinating conjunction **_that_** can often be omitted.
>
> _I think **that he'll succeed**._
> _I think **he'll succeed**._

Adverbial clauses

Adverbial clauses generally follow the main clause unless otherwise stated. The following are the main types of adverbial clause:

Time: sets the timing for the main clause.

> We should go **as soon as you are ready**.
> I'll call for you **whenever you like**.
> **Since she went away**, I haven't been able to sleep.
> **The moment he said it**, I started to feel better.

– may come before or after the main clause.

– introduced by *after, as, as soon as, before, once, since, till, the moment (that), until, whenever, when, while*.

Place: sets where the action of the main clause takes place.

> I put it **where nobody would find it**.
> He made an impact **everywhere that he went**.
> **Wherever you looked**, he was to be found.

– introduced by *where, wherever,* or *everywhere*.

Manner: sets out how the main clause was carried out.

– introduced by *as, as if, as though, how, just as,* or *the way that*.

> Mandy looked **as if she had seen a ghost**.
> Cameron wandered in, **the way that he does**.
> You have to fasten it **as though it was a shoelace**.
> The room was decorated **just as he had imagined**.

Reason: sets out the thinking behind the action of the main clause.

> I don't want to go **because I'm not keen on old movies**.
> **Since no one was ready**, I sat down and turned on the TV.

– may come before or after the main clause.

– introduced by *as*, *because*, or *since*.

Purpose: sets out what it was hoped would be achieved by carrying out the action of the main clause.

> Put it just there **so that it holds the door open**.
> Leave a bit for Becky **in case she's hungry when she gets in**.

– introduced by *so that*, *in order that*, *in case*, or *lest*.

• Purpose can also be indicated by *so as to*, *in order to* followed by the base form of a verb.

> I'm living with my mum and dad **so as to save money**.
> He put the chair against the door **in order to hold it open**.

Result: sets out what happened when the main clause was carried out.

> Ben was **so** angry **that he kicked the wall hard**.
> Nina is **such a** generous person **that she's often short of money**.

– introduced by *so* + **adjective/adverb** + *that* or by *such a* + **noun phrase** + *that*.

Contrast: suggests that something else may need to be taken into account regarding the main clause.

> ***However much you may want to spend your money**, try to save a little each month.*
> ***Although it had rained**, the ground was still very dry.*
> *We must try to do something for the environment, **even if we can't solve all the world's problems**.*

– may come before or after the main clause.

– introduced by *although, even though, even if, however, much as,* or *while.*

Relative clauses

Relative clauses tell us more about nouns. They function rather like adjectives, and are found as **postmodifiers** in a noun phrase. The noun that is modified is called the **antecedent**. Relative clauses normally begin with **who**, **whom**, **whose**, or **that**.

These words are called **relative pronouns**. Note that some of them also function as interrogative pronouns. See also p. 211.

A relative pronoun can be the subject

> The people **who live upstairs** are having a party.
> The dog **that bit me** had to be put down.

or object

> I don't like the music **that they are playing**.
> A man **whom I met on holiday** phoned last might.

of the verb in the relative clause. If it is the object, it can be left out in ordinary informal speech and writing.

> I don't like the music **they are playing**.
> A man **I met on holiday** phoned last night.

Subject and object relative pronouns come at the beginning of the relative clause.

- A relative pronoun can also be the object of a preposition.

> It was definitely Diana **to whom she was referring**.
> It's a great game **at which anyone can excel**.

In informal English a relative clause can end in a preposition, especially if the relative pronoun is omitted.

> *It was definitely Diana* **(that)** *she was referring to*.
> *It's great game* **(which)** *anyone can excel at*.

Defining and non-defining relative clauses

There are two sorts of relative clause.

Some relative clauses act rather like an adjective by providing more information about a particular noun.

> *The people* **who live upstairs** *are having a party*.
> *I don't like the music* **that they're playing**.
> *The girl* **who was on the bus with us** *is called Sonia*.

These are called **defining** relative clauses or **restrictive** relative clauses. A defining relative clause is never separated from the noun by a comma.

The other type of relative clause adds extra information to the whole of the main clause. These are **non-defining relative clauses** or **non-restrictive** relative clauses. This type of clause is separated from the main clause by commas.

> *The man next door,* **who works from home**, *kept an eye on the house for us*.
> *Thomas went home early,* **which was a relief to us all**.
> *We stopped in Dryburgh,* **which is a good place for a picnic**.

Compare:

Defining.
My brother who lives in Canada is a lawyer.
(There are several brothers. The Canadian one is a lawyer.)

Non-defining.
My brother, who lives in Canada, is a lawyer.
(There is only one brother. He is a lawyer. He happens to
   live in Canada.)

Conditional clauses

Conditional sentences consist of a main clause and a **conditional clause** (sometimes called an *if-clause*). The conditional clause usually begins with *if* or *unless*. The conditional clause can come before or after the main clause.

> We'll be late **if we don't leave now**.
> We'll be late **unless we leave now**.
> **If we don't leave now**, we'll be late.
> **Unless we leave now**, we'll be late.

There are three main types of conditional sentence.

Type 1

The main clause uses **will**, **can**, **may**, or **might** + the **base form** of a main verb. The *if-clause* uses the present simple tense.

> **If you take the first bus**, you'll get there on time.
> She'll be cold **if she doesn't wear a coat**.
> **If you need more helpers**, I can try and get some time off work.

Type 1 sentences refer to the future. They suggest that the action in the main clause is quite likely to happen.

> They **will** not finish their homework unless they start now.
> If you book early, you **will** get a seat.

The use of the modal verb *may* or *might* in the main clause suggests that there is some doubt whether the main verb action will be achieved.

> If you book early, you **may** get a seat.
> Mary **might** deliver your parcel, if you ask her.

Type 2

The main clause uses **would**, **could**, or **might** + the **base form** of a main verb. The **if-clause** uses the past simple tense

> If Jim **lent** us his car, we could go to the party.
> We would save £3.50 a day if we **didn't eat** any lunch.
> If burglars **broke** into my house, they wouldn't find any money.
> Would you be very angry if I **failed** my exam?

or the past subjunctive.

> If I **were you**, I'd phone her straight away.

Type 2 sentences refer to an imaginary situation. They imply that the action in the **if-clause** will probably not happen.

> If I won the lottery, I would buy a house in France.
> (...but I don't think I'll win the lottery.)
> If you didn't spend all your money on lottery tickets, you could afford a holiday.
> (...but you do spend all your money on lottery tickets.)

The past subjunctive is often used when giving advice to someone, especially about what the person should do.

> If I **were you**, I'd tell them the truth.

Type 3

The main clause uses **would**, **could**, or **might** + **have** + the **past participle** of a main verb. The **if-clause** uses the past perfect tense.

> We could have had a longer holiday, if we **hadn't spent** so much money on the house.
> If I **had known** about the exam, I would have paid more attention in class.

In Type 3 sentences the speaker is looking back from the present to a past time and event. The speaker is talking about what might have happened but did not, either because the wrong thing was done or because nothing was done. This type of sentence is used when making excuses, showing regret, blaming, or giving an explanation.

Conditional clauses can also be used to talk about consequences, or to give an opinion about a situation in the following ways:

– The *if-clause* uses the present simple tense and the main clause uses the present simple tense. This is used to refer to universal truths.

> *If you **heat** water to 100°C, it **boils**.*
> *Plants **die** if they **don't get** enough water.*

– The *if-clause* uses the present simple tense and the main clause is in the imperative. This is used to give advice or orders for particular situations or sets of circumstances.

> *If the alarm **goes off**, **make** your way outside to the car park.*
> *If a red light **shows** here, **switch off** the machine.*

– The *if-clause* uses the present continuous or present simple tense and the main clause uses a modal verb. This is used to make suggestions and give advice.

> *If you**'re thinking of** buying a lawnmower, you **could** try mine first.*
> *You **should** turn down his radio if you **don't want** the neighbours to complain.*

– The *if-clause* uses **will/would** and the main clause uses a modal verb.

This is used to make a request or to give a polite order.

> *If **you'll** wait a minute, the doctor **can** see you.*
> *If you **would** sign here, please, **I'll** be able to send you the books.*

> Note that a *'d* in the main clause is the contracted form of
> *would*. However, a *'d* in an *if*-clause is the contracted form
> of *had*.
>
> *I'd have gone if **he'd** invited me.*
> *I **would** have gone **if he had invited me**.*
> *I **would've** gone if **he'd** invited me.*

In the main clause the contracted forms of the modals used in speech
and informal writing are:

I'd have	or	**I would've**
I could've		**I might've**

Reporting speech

There are two ways of writing down or reporting what was said on any occasion. We can repeat the actual words used (**direct speech**),

> Monica said, **'There's nothing we can do about it.'**

or we can build the words into our own sentences (**reported speech**).

> Monica said that there was nothing we could do about it.

The words reported are normally accompanied by a **reporting verb**.

> Monica **said/declared** that there was nothing we could
>   do about it.
> 'There is nothing we can do about it,' Monica **replied**.

Another name for reported speech is **indirect speech**.

Direct speech

Direct speech gives the actual words that the speaker used. It is common in novels and other writing where the actual words of a speaker are quoted.

> Monica said, **'There's nothing we can do about it.'**

The **reporting verb** may come before the words that were actually spoken, or after them, or at a natural pause inside the reported sentence.

> **Monica said,** 'There is nothing we can do about it.'
> 'There is nothing we can do about it,' **Monica said**.
> 'It's no good,' **Monica said,** 'we'll just have to ask for help.'

- The comma comes inside the quotation marks, unless the reporting verb is positioned inside a reported sentence that itself does not require a comma.

    There is', Monica said, 'nothing we can do about it.'

- Typical reporting verbs are: *agree, answer, ask, inquire, explain, say, tell,* and *wonder.*

The subject and the reporting verb are sometimes reversed.

    'There is nothing we can do about it,' **said Monica**.

The actual words spoken always begin with a capital letter, unless the reporting verb comes within a sentence. They are separated from the reporting verb by a comma, unless they are followed by a question mark or an exclamation.

    'Why did you do it?' she asked.
    'Oh, mind your own business!' he snapped.

- The words spoken are enclosed in inverted commas (single or double quotation marks).

    'Have you been to the new shopping mall yet?' *enquired Shona.*

    "I've already seen it," *John replied.*

- Single quotation marks are often used to draw attention to a word that is being mentioned for a particular purpose. (See also p. 296.)

    There is no such word as 'fubber'.
    He called me a 'stubborn old goat'.

Reported speech

Reported speech or **indirect speech** reports something that was said, but does not use the actual words that the speaker uttered.

> **Lynn asked** whether Pippa had been to the new shopping mall.
> **Pippa replied** that she hadn't, but **she had heard** that there
>   were some really cool shops there.

Reported speech always has two clauses. The words that are spoken are put in a **reported clause**. There is also a **main clause** that contains a **reporting verb**. The main clause with the reporting verb usually comes before the **reported clause**.

> **Katie told me** that Alison is going to resign.
> **Peter asked** whether Mandy was feeling better.

The reporting verb in the main clause tells us how the sentence was uttered, e.g. *comment, remark, say, tell*. If the reported clause is a **statement**, the main clause is linked to the reported clause by *that*.

> Mary said **that** her favourite actor was Ben Whishaw.
> John replied **that** he preferred Scarlett Johansson.

If the reported clause asks a question, the main verb will be a question verb e.g. *ask, inquire, wonder, query*. The link between the main clause and the reported clause will be *if* or **whether**.

> Amy asked Jo **if** she had seen the movie.
> Will enquired **whether** the documents were ready.

• The linking word **that** can be left out after most reporting verbs,

> Jamie told Dad **(that)** he had passed his driving test.
> Lucy said Alan had been accepted at drama school.

but the links **if** or **whether** cannot be left out.

> *Miriam asked **if** she could borrow Leonie's mp3 player.*
> *Evelyn wondered **whether** the concert would be sold out.*

- Speech in a reported clause is not separated from the reporting verb by a comma, is not enclosed in inverted commas, and does not begin with a capital letter unless it is a proper noun. Reported questions are not followed by question marks.

An alternative position for main clauses that would normally have a linking *that*, is after the reported clause. In this case, the link is left out.

> *Harry Potter was on that night, **Mary said**.*

> Reported clauses can also be used to express what is in someone's mind as well as what is actually spoken.
>
> > *Evelyn **wondered** whether **the concert would be sold out**.*
> > *Charlotte **thought** that **she had better go and see her family**.*

Changes in the reported words

When you use reported speech, the words put into the reported clause do not exactly match the words actually spoken.

> *'I'll leave here at 8.30 on Friday.'*
> *She says **that she will leave home at 8.30 on Friday**.*
> *'I'm looking forward to seeing you.'*
> *She says **she's looking forward to seeing us**.*

Pronouns and **possessive determiners** have to change in reported speech because of the change of speaker, e.g. *I* may become *she*; *you* may become *us* or *him*.

'I believe you.'
*She said that **she** believed **us**.*

'I'm leaving you.'
*She said that **she** was leaving **him**.*

'I've finished.'
*She said that **she had finished**.*

Expressions of place and time may also have to change, e.g. *here* may become *there* or *home*; *Friday* may become *in three days' time*.

'I've been here before.'
*She said that she **had been there before**.*

'I'll see you on Monday.'
*She said that she would see him **in three days' time**.*

The tense in reported clauses

The verb may also change, e.g. *must* becomes *had to* in reported speech. The most common change is a change of tense.

'Hello Jake? It's me, Penny. I've arrived here on time, and I'm
going to take a bus to your place. There's one coming now,
so I'd better run.'

*She rang to say that **she'd** arrived **there** on time and **was going
to** take a bus to **our** place. Then she said that one **was
coming at that very moment**, so **she had to** run.*

A reporting verb in the present tense can be used in the main clause when you report on a letter or on a recent conversation, e.g. a telephone conversation.

'Hello, Jake? I've arrived here on time, and I'm going to take a
bus to your place.'
*Penny has just phoned. She **says** that she has arrived on time*
*and that **she's coming** here by bus.*

However, it is more common to use a past tense when reporting speech.

The changes of tense may be summarized as follows:

direct speech	reported speech
present simple	past simple
present continuous	past continuous
present perfect	past perfect
present perfect continuous	past perfect continuous
past simple	past perfect or past simple
future	conditional

Questions

Verb tenses in reported questions undergo the same changes as in statements. See p. 279.

'Are you ready?'
*He asked (us) if/whether we **were** ready.*

'What time is it?'
*He asked what time it **was**.*
'Where has Jim gone?'
*He wanted to know where Jim **had gone**.*

Reporting verbs for questions include *ask, inquire, want to know,* and *wonder.*

Direct **yes/no** questions are linked to the reporting clause by **if** or **whether**. **WH-** question words, e.g. *who, when, where*, are used in both direct and indirect questions.

> *'Are you ready?'*
> *He asked (us) if/whether we **were** ready.*

> *'What time is it?'*
> *He asked what time it **was**.*
> *'Where has Jim gone?'*
> *He wanted to know where Jim **had gone**.*

- The word order in a reported question is the same as that of a direct statement. Question order is not used in reported speech, i.e. no part of the verb comes before the subject.

Orders and requests

Orders are reported with **tell** + **object** + **to infinitive**.

> *'Stop calling me names!'*
> *She **told him to stop** calling her names.*

Requests for action are reported with **ask** + **object** + **to infinitive**.

> *'Please don't leave your things on the floor.'*
> *She asked us **not to leave** our things on the floor.*

Requests for objects are reported with **ask for** + **object**.

> *'Can I have the salt, please?'*
> *He **asked for the salt**.*

- The reporting verb can be used in the passive.

> *'Don't park here, please; it's reserved for the doctors.'*
> *I was **told not to park** there.*

Suggestions, advice, promises, etc.

A variety of verbs can be used for reporting suggestions and similar types of speech. Some of these are:

— *suggest, insist on* + present participle

> 'Let's go to the zoo.'
> **He suggested going to the zoo.**

— *advise, invite, warn* + direct object + **not** + **to** infinitive

> 'I wouldn't buy that one, if I were you.'
> She advised me **not to buy** that one.

— *refuse, threaten* + **to** infinitive

> 'I'm not telling you!'
> She **refused to tell** me.

— *offer, promise* + **to** infinitive

> 'Don't worry; I'll help you.'
> He **promised to help** me.

Punctuation

The apostrophe (')

Misusing or omitting the apostrophe is one of the commonest punctuation errors.

Showing possession

The apostrophe (') is used to show that something belongs to someone. It is usually added to the end of a word and followed by an -*s*.

- **-'s** is added to the end of singular words.

    a baby's pushchair
    Hannah's book
    a child's cry

- **-'s** is added to the end of plural words not ending in -*s*.

    children's games
    women's clothes
    people's lives

- An apostrophe alone (') is added to plural words ending in -*s*.

    Your grandparents are your parents' parents.
    We're campaigning for workers' rights.
    They've hired a new ladies' fashion guru.

- **-'s** is added to the end of names and singular words ending in -*s*.

    James's car
    the octopus's tentacles

- -'s is added to the end of certain professions or occupations to indicate workplaces.

    She's on her way to the doctor's.
    James is at the hairdresser's.

- -'s is added to the end of people or their names to indicate that you are talking about their home.

    I'm going over to Harry's for tea tonight.
    I popped round to Mum's this afternoon, but she wasn't in.

- Note that if the word is a classical Greek name, or a historical figure or building, an apostrophe only is sometimes preferred.

    Dickens' novels
    St Giles' Cathedral

-'s can also be added to:

- whole phrases

    My next-door neighbour's dog was barking away like mad.
    John and Cath's house was on TV last night.

- indefinite pronouns such as *somebody* or *anywhere*

    Is this anybody's pencil case?
    It's nobody's fault but mine.

- each other

    We're getting used to each other's habits.
    We kept forgetting each other's names.

When the possessor is an inanimate object (rather than a living thing), the apostrophe is not used and the word order is changed.

> *the middle of the street* (not *the street's middle*)
> *the front of the house* (not *the house's front*)

To test whether an apostrophe is in the right place, think about who the owner is.

> *the boy's books* [= *the books belonging to the boy*]
> *the boys' books* [= *the books belonging to the boys*]

Note that:

– An apostrophe is *not* used to form possessive pronouns such as *its*, *yours*, or *theirs*.

– An apostrophe is *not* used to form the plurals of words such as *potatoes* or *tomatoes*.

With letters and numbers

An apostrophe is used in front of two figures referring to a year or decade.

> *French students rioted in* **'68** [*short for* '1968'].
> *He worked as a schoolteacher during the* **'60s** *and early* **'90s**.

An apostrophe can be used in plurals of letters and numbers to make them more readable.

> *Mind your p's and q's.*
> *His 2's look a bit like 7's.*
> *She got straight A's in her exams.*

> REMEMBER
>
> it's = it is, e.g. *It's a holiday today.*
> its = belonging to it, e.g. *The dog was scratching its ear.*

Contracted forms

An apostrophe is used in shortened forms of words to show that one or more letters have been missed out. Contractions are usually shortened forms of auxiliary verbs

be	**have**
I'**m**	I/we/they'**ve** (have)
We/you/they'**re** (are)	He/she/it/one'**s** (has)
He/she/it/one'**s** (is)	I/we/you/he/she/it/one/they'**d** (had)

would
I/we/you/he/she/it/one/they'**d** (would)

or the negative *not*.

not
*We/you/they aren***'t**
*He/she/it/one isn***'t**
*I/we/they haven***'t**
*He/she/it/one hasn***'t**

In order to work out what the contracted forms '**s** and '**d** represent, you need to look at what follows it:

– If '**s** is followed by an *-ing* form, it represents the auxiliary *is*.

> She'**s reading** *a book about the ancient Egyptians.*
> He'**s going** *to Ibiza for his holidays.*

– If **'s** is followed by an adjective or a noun phrase, it represents the main verb *is*.

> She**'s nervous** about meeting my parents.
> He**'s brilliant** at maths.

– If **'s** is followed by a past participle, it can represent *is* as it is used in the passive,

> He**'s portrayed** by the media as a kindly old grandfather.
> It**'s** often **said** that rock stars are frustrated actors.

or *has* as it is used in the present perfect.

> She**'s broken** her wrist.
> It**'s been** ages since we last saw you.

– If **'s** is followed by *got*, it represents the auxiliary *has*.

> She**'s got** two brothers and one sister.
> It**'s got** everything you could want.

– If **'d** is followed by a past participle, it represents the auxiliary *had*.

> I**'d raced** against him before, but never in a marathon.
> She couldn't believe what she**'d done**.

– If **'d** is followed by a base form, it represents the modal auxiliary *would*.

> I**'d give up** now, if I were you.
> When we were kids we**'d spend** hours out on our bikes.

– If **'d** is followed by *rather* or *better*, it represents the modal auxiliary *would*.

> We**'d better** go home soon.
> I**'d rather** not talk about that.

The comma (,)

The comma marks a short pause between elements in a sentence.

Separating main clauses

Main clauses that are joined together with *and* or *but* do not normally have a comma before the conjunction unless the two clauses have different subjects.

> *You go out of the door and turn immediately left.*
> *It was cold outside, but we decided to go out for a walk anyway.*

Separating subordinate clauses from main clauses

Commas are normally used if the subordinate clause comes before the main clause.

> *If you have any problems, just call me.*
> *Just call me if you have any problems.*

Sometimes a comma is used even when the main clause comes first, if the clauses are particularly long.

> *We should be able to finish the work by the end of the week, if nothing unexpected turns up between now and then.*

Separating relative clauses from main clauses

Commas are used to mark off non-defining relative clauses (see p. 271). This is the type of clause that adds to information about a noun or noun phrase.

> *My next-door neighbour, who works from home, is keeping an*
> *eye on the house while we're away.*
> *She moved to Los Angeles, where she was immediately signed*
> *as a singer songwriter.*

Commas are not required in defining relative clauses (see p. 270), since these simply postmodify the noun.

> *Let's make sure the money goes to the people **who need it most**.*
> *The computer **(that) I borrowed** kept on crashing.*

Separating items in a list

Commas are used to separate three or more items in a list or series.

> *She got out bread, butter, and jam (but bread and butter).*

Note that the comma is often not given before the final *and* or *or*.

> *They breed dogs, cats, rabbits and hamsters.*
> *We did canoeing, climbing and archery.*

Separating adjectives

Commas are used between adjectives, whether they come before the noun (i.e. used attributively) or after a linking verb (i.e. used predicatively).

> *It was a hot, dry and dusty road.*
> *It's wet, cold and windy outside.*

A comma is not usually used before an adjective that is followed by *and*.

With adverbials

When an adverbial such as *however*, *therefore* or *unfortunately* modifies a whole sentence, it is separated from the rest of the sentence by a comma.

> *However, police would not confirm this rumour.*
> *Therefore, I try to avoid using the car as much as possible.*

With question tags and short responses

Commas are used before question tags and after *yes* or *no* in short responses.

> *It's quite cold today, isn't it?*
> *He's up to date with all his injections, isn't he?*
> *Are you the mother of these children? – Yes, I am.*
> *You're Amy Osborne, aren't you? – No, I'm not.*

With vocatives

Commas are used to separate the name of a person or group being addressed from the rest of the sentence.

> *And now, ladies and gentlemen, please raise your glasses in*
>   *a toast to the happy couple.*
> *Come on, Olivia, be reasonable.*
> *Dad, can you come and help me, please?*

With discourse markers

Commas are used to separate discourse markers like *Well* and *Now then* from the rest of the sentence.

> *Well, believe it or not, I actually passed!*
> *Now then, let's see what's on TV tonight.*
> *Actually, I quite enjoyed it.*

In reported speech

Commas are used to follow direct speech (if there is no question or exclamation mark after the quotation), or to show that it comes next.

> *'I don't understand this question,' said Peter.*
> *Peter said, 'I don't understand this question.'*
> *'You're crazy!' Claire exclaimed.*
> *'What do you think you're doing?' Dad bellowed.*

It is also possible to punctuate reported speech of the type *Peter said, '...'* using a colon instead of a comma. This is a particularly common practice in American English.

> *Peter said: 'Dream on.'*

In dates

A comma must be used between the day of the month and the year, when the two numbers are next to each other.

> *March 31, 2011*

Quotation marks (' ') or (" ")

Direct speech

Direct speech gives the actual words that a speaker used. It is common in novels and other writing where the actual words of a speaker are quoted (see p. 278).

The words spoken are enclosed in single or double quotation marks.

> **'Have you been to the new shopping precinct yet?'**
> *enquired Shona.*

> **"I've already seen it,"** *John replied.*

• The comma comes inside the quotation marks, unless the reporting verb is positioned inside a reported sentence that itself does not require a comma.

> *'There is'*, *Monica said*, *'nothing we can do about it.'*

Other uses

Single quotation marks are sometimes used:

– to draw attention to a word

> *The word* **'book'** *can be used as a noun or a verb.*

– to indicate an unusual use of a word

> *She pointed out that websites used for internet voting could*
> *be* **'spoofed'**.

- to suggest that the writer want to be distanced from a word.

     I don't agree with this **'mercy killing'** *business.*

- Note that the full stop comes after the quotation marks in such cases.

Capital letters

A capital (or 'upper case') letter is used to mark the beginning of a sentence.

> *When I was 20, I dropped out of university and became a model.*

Capital letters are also used for the first letter in proper nouns. These include:

– people's names

> *Jenny Forbes*   *William Davidson*

– days of the week

> *Wednesday*   *Saturday*

– months of the year

> *August*   *January*

– public holidays

> *Christmas*   *Yom Kippur*

– nationalities

> *Spanish*   *Iraqi*

– languages

> *Swahili*   *Flemish*

- geographical locations

  Australia   *Loch Ness*
  Mount Everest   *The Mediterranean Sea*

- company names

  Dyson   *Harper Collins*

- religions

  Islam   *Buddhism*

Capital letters are also used for the first letter in titles of books, magazines, newspapers, TV shows, films, etc. Where there are several words, a capital letter is usually used for all the main content words in the title (i.e. not the prepositions or the determiners – unless they are the first word in the title).

  The Times   *Hello!*
  Twelfth Night   *The Secret Garden*
  Newsnight   *Mamma Mia!*

The full stop (.)

Full stops are used:

– to mark the end of a sentence

> *Let's have some lunch.*
> *I have to catch a bus in ten minutes.*

– to mark the end of a sentence fragment

> *Are you cold? – Yes, a bit.*
> *Do you like this sort of music? Not really.*

– in initials for people's names, although this practice is becoming less frequent

> *J.K. Rowling*   *Iain M. Banks*
> *M.C. Hammer*   *Ronald G. Hardie*

– after abbreviations, although this practice is becoming less frequent.

> *P.S. Do pop in next time you're passing.*
> *She's moved to the I.T. department*
> *R.S.V.P. to Helen Douglas on 01234 676240.*
> *The U.S. government reacted strongly to the accusation.*

When an abbreviation consists of a shortened word such as *Re.* or *Prof.*, a full stop is needed.

> *Re. your suggestion that we shorten the lunch hour, could*
>   *we arrange a quick meeting to discuss the various options?*
> *Prof. John Johansson will be speaking on the subject of*
>   *'Discourse in the Electronic Age'.*
> *Flight BA 345: dep. 09.44 arr. 11.10.*

When an abbreviation contains the last letter of the shortened word, a full stop is not needed.

> **Dr** McDonald **St** Mary's School
> 41, Douglas **Rd** Universal Pictures (UK) **Ltd**

- Note that full stops are not used in many common sets of initials,

> *Did you see that programme on **BBC** 2 last night?*
> *The government has promised more funding for the **NHS**.*

or at the end of headlines, headings and titles.

> *Fear grips global stock markets*
> *Teaching grammar as a liberating force*
> *Wuthering Heights*

Remember that a full stop, and not a question mark, is used after an indirect question or a polite request.

> *He asked if the bus had left.*
> *Will you open your books on page 14.*
> *I wonder what's happened.*
> *She asked him where he was going.*

> In American English, the full stop is called a period.

The question mark (?)

The question mark marks the end of a question.

> *When will we be arriving?*
> *Why did you do that?*
> *Does any of this matter?*
> *He's certain to be elected, isn't he?*

Question marks are used in direct questions, i.e. when the actual words of a speaker are used. A reported question should end with a full stop.

> *The lady said, 'Where are you going?'*
> *The lady asked where she was going.*

Note that you put a question mark at the end of a question, even if the words in the sentence are not in the normal question order, or some words are omitted. Care is needed here as such a sentence can look, at first sight, like a statement rather than a question.

> *You know he doesn't live here any longer?*

A full stop, rather than a question mark, is used after an indirect question.

> *I'd like to know what you've been doing all this time.*
> *I wonder what's happened.*

A full stop also replaces a question mark at the end of a sentence which looks like a question if, in fact, it is really a polite request.

> *Will you please return the completed forms to me.*
> *Would you please call my brother and ask him to collect my car.*

The exclamation mark (!)

The exclamation mark is used after exclamations and emphatic expressions.

> *I can't believe it!*
> *Oh, no! Look at this mess!*

The exclamation mark loses its effect if it is overused. It is better to use a full stop after a sentence expressing mild excitement or humour.

> *It was such a beautiful day.*
> *I felt like a perfect banana.*

The colon (:)

The colon indicates a break between two main clauses which is stronger than a comma but weaker than a full stop.

A colon is used:

– in front of a list

> *I used three colours: green, blue and pink.*
> *Make sure you wear clothes made from natural fibres:*
> *cotton, silk and wool.*

– in front of an explanation or a reason

> *Nevertheless, the main problem remained: what should*
> *be done with the two men?*
> *I decided against going away this weekend: the weather*
> *forecast was dreadful.*

– after introductory headings

> *Cooking time: about five minutes.*
> *Start time: 10 o'clock.*

– in more formal writing, between two main clauses that are connected

> *It made me feel claustrophobic: what, I wonder, would happen*
> *to someone who was really unable to tolerate being locked*
> *into such a tiny space?*
> *Be patient: the next book in the series has not yet been*
> *published.*

- in front of the second part of a book title

  Farming and wildlife: a study in compromise
  Beyond single words: the most frequent collocations in spoken
    English.

- to introduce direct speech, especially in American English, or when the quotation is particularly long.

  He said: 'You owe me three dollars and twenty-five cents.'
  The Health Minister said: 'The NHS I.T. programme will mean
    that patients will get access to more comprehensive
    information to help them make choices.'

The semicolon (;)

The semicolon is used to mark a break between two main clauses when there is a balance or a contrast between the clauses.

> Compare:

> *The engine roared into life. The propellers began to turn.*
> *The plane taxied down the runway ready for takeoff.*

> with:

> *The engine roared into life; the propellers began to turn;*
>   *the plane taxied down the runway ready for takeoff.*

A useful test to work out when to use a semicolon is to ask yourself whether the two clauses could be written instead as separate sentences. If the answer is 'yes', then you can use a semicolon.

Note that it is quite acceptable to use a full stop in these cases, but a semicolon is preferable if you wish to convey the sense of a link or continuity between the clauses in your narrative.

> *I'm not that interested in jazz; I prefer classical music.*
> *He knew everything about me; I had never even heard of him.*

A semicolon is also used to separate items in a list, especially if the listed items are phrases or clauses, which may already contain commas.

> *The holiday was a disaster: the flight was four hours late;*
>   *the hotel, which was described as 'luxury', was dirty;*
>   *and it rained for the whole fortnight.*

Brackets ( )

Brackets (also called **parentheses**) are used to enclose a word or words which can be left out and still leave a meaningful sentence.

> *The wooded area (see map below) is approximately*
> *4,000 hectares.*
> *This is a process which Hayek (a writer who came to*
> *rather different conclusions) also observed.*

Brackets are also used to show alternatives or options.

> *Any student(s) interested in taking part should e-mail me.*
> *A goat should give from three to six pints (1.7 to 3.4 litres)*
> *of milk a day.*

Note that when the structure of the sentence as a whole demands punctuation after a bracketed section, the punctuation is given *outside* the brackets.

> *I haven't yet spoken to John (I mean John Maple, my boss),*
> *but I have a meeting with him on Friday.*
> *For lunch we had sandwiches (pastrami on rye and so on),*
> *salami, coleslaw, fried chicken, and potato salad.*

Punctuation is given before the closing brackets only when it applies to the bracketed section rather than to the sentence as a whole.

> *He's very handsome (positively gorgeous in fact!) and still*
> *single.*

Square brackets [ ]

Square brackets are used, usually in books and articles, when supplying words that make a quotation clearer or that comment on it, although they were not originally said or written.

> *Mr Runcie concluded: 'The novel is at its strongest when describing the dignity of Cambridge [a slave] and the education of Emily [the daughter of an absentee landlord].'*

The hyphen (-)

The hyphen joins words or parts of words.

Hyphens are used at the ends of lines where a word has been split, to warn the reader that the word continues on the next line. If the word you need to split is clearly made up of two or more smaller words or elements, you should put the hyphen after the first of these parts. Otherwise, you put the hyphen at the end of a syllable.

> *wheel-barrow*   *inter-national*
> *listen-ing*   *compli-mentary*
> *infor-mation*

It is best not to add a hyphen if the word is a short one, or if it would mean writing just one or two letters at the end or beginning of a line. For example, it would be better to write 'unnatural' on the line below, rather than writing 'un-' on one line and 'natural' on the next.

Prefixes that are used in front of a word beginning with a capital letter always have a hyphen after them.

> *a wave of anti-British feeling*
> *a neo-Byzantine cathedral*

A hyphen is used to join two or more words that together form an adjective, where this adjective is used *before* the noun it describes.

> *an up-to-date account*
> *a last-minute rush*
> *a six-year-old boy*

The hyphen is omitted when the adjective so formed comes after the noun or pronoun it describes.

The accounts are up to date.
It was all rather last minute.
He's six years old.

Some common compound nouns are usually written with hyphens.

mother-in-law   *great-grandmother*

Hyphens can be used to split words that have been formed by adding a prefix to another word, especially to avoid an awkward combination of letters or confusion with another word.

re-elect
re-covering furniture
re-creation

The dash (–)

A spaced dash (i.e. with a single space before and after it) is used:

– at the beginning and end of a comment that interrupts the flow of a sentence.

> *Now children – Kenneth, stop that immediately! – open your books on page 20.*

– to separate off extra information.

> *Boots and shoes – all shapes, sizes and colours – tumbled out.*

An unspaced dash (i.e. with no space before or after it) is used:

– to indicate a range.

> *pages 26–42*

– between two adjectives or noun modifiers that indicate that two countries or groups are involved in something or that an individual has two roles or aspects.

> *Swedish–Norwegian relations improved,*
> *the United States–Canada free trade pact*
> *a mathematician–philosopher*

– to indicate that something such as a plane or a train goes between two places.

> *the Anguilla–St Kitts flight*
> *the New York–Montreal train*

The slash (/)

The slash separates letters, words or numbers. It is used to indicate alternatives, ratios and ranges, and in website addresses.

> *he/she/it*
> *200 km/hr*
> *the 2001/02 accounting year*
> *http://www.abcdefg.com*

Punctuation in numbers

Dates

Full stops or slashes are often used in dates.

	American usage
12.3.09	3/12/09
2.28.15	2/28/15

Scientific usage

Full stops are not used in scientific abbreviations.

12 kg	50 cm

Times

Full stops and occasionally colons are used in times.

| 4.15 p.m. | 21.15 |
| 3:30 a.m. | 20:30 |

Long numbers

Commas are used in numbers to mark off units of thousands and millions.

1,359	2,543,678

Decimals

Full stops indicate decimal points.

1.5   25.08